ENLIGHTENMENT
EDINBURGH
A GUIDE

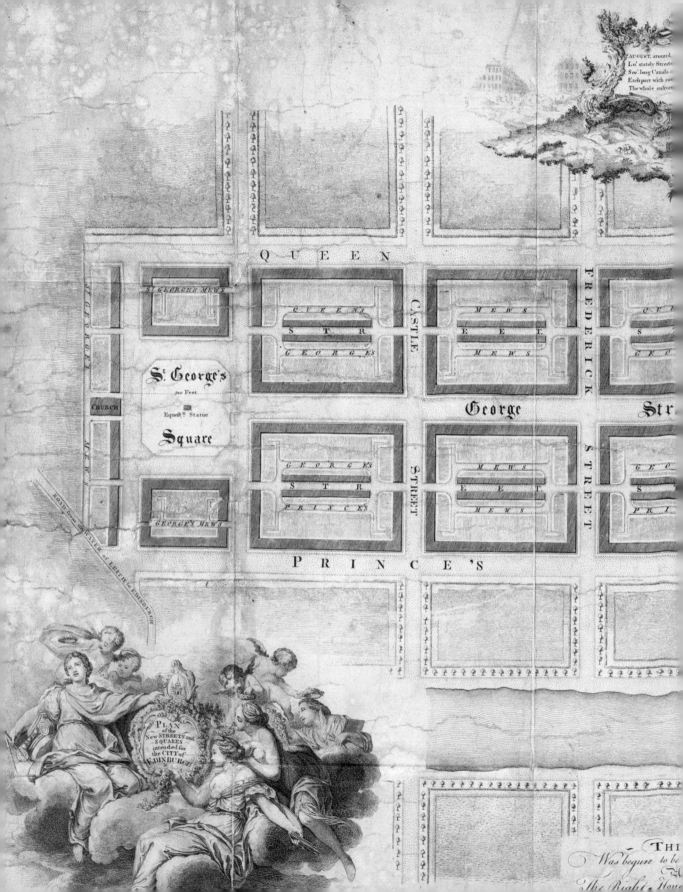

QUEEN

St GEORGE'S MEWS

CASTLE

MEWS

STREET

FREDERICK

QUEEN'S
S T R.
GEORGE'S

MEWS

E E T.

MEWS

St
GEO

St. George's

500 Feet

Equest.n Statue

Square

CHURCH

George

Str

GEORGE'S
S T R.
PRINCES

MEWS
E E T.
MEWS

GEO
S
PR

MEWS

ROAD from WATER OF LEITH to EDINBURGH

GEORGE'S MEWS

PRINCE'S

AUGUST, around,
Lo! stately Streets
See! long Canals
Each part with
The whole enliven

PLAN
of the
New STREETS and
SQUARES
intended for
the CITY of
EDINBURGH

THI
Was begun to be
The Right Hon

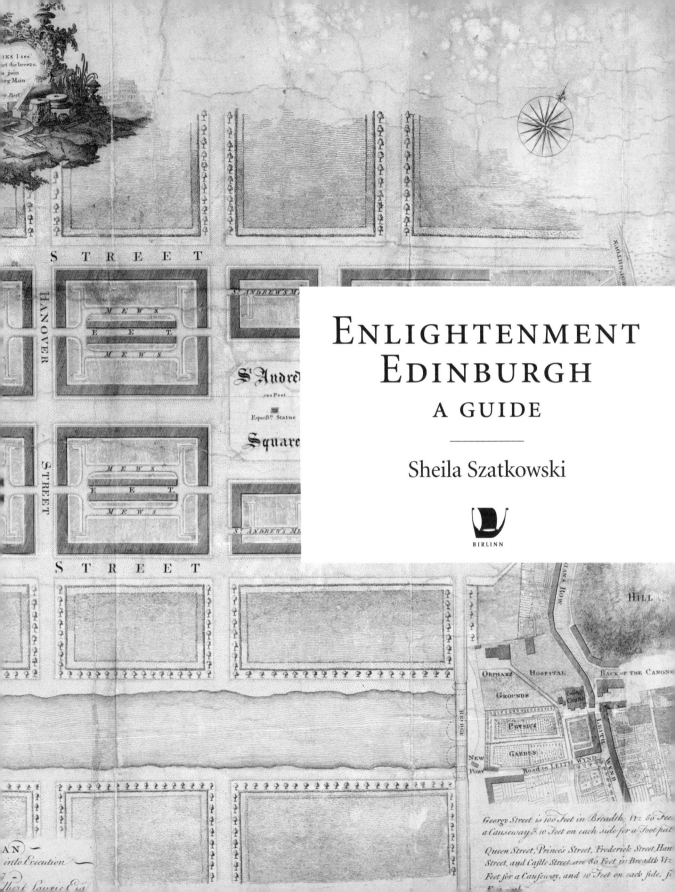

Enlightenment Edinburgh

A GUIDE

Sheila Szatkowski

BIRLINN

First published in Great Britain in 2017 by
Birlinn Ltd
West Newington House
10 Newington Road
Edinburgh EH9 1QS

www.birlinn.co.uk

ISBN 978 1 78027 373 0

Copyright © Sheila Szatkowski 2017

Photography by Josef Szatkowski
Half-title map: W. Edgar: Plan of the City and Castle of
Edinburgh 1765 (detail)
Title-page map: J. Craig: Plan of the new streets and
squares, included for his ancient capital of North Britain,
1768 (detail)
Chapter-opening maps show details from W. Edgar:
Plan of the City and Castle of Edinburgh 1765 (chapter 1)
and R. Kirkwood: Plan of the City of Edinburgh
and its environs 1817 (chapters 2–8)
All reproduced by permission of the Trustees of the
National Library of Scotland
Modern maps drawn by Jim Lewis

The right of Sheila Szatkowski to be identified
as the author of this work has been asserted by
her in accordance with the Copyright, Designs
and Patents Act, 1988

All rights reserved.

No part of this publication may be reproduced, stored,
or transmitted in any form, or by any means, electronic,
mechanical or photocopying, recording or otherwise,
without the express written permission of the publisher.

British Library Cataloguing-in-Publication Data
A catalogue record for this book is available on
request from the British Library

Designed and typeset by Mark Blackadder

Unless otherwise stated all illustrations and
photographs are from the author's private collection

Printed and bound by Gutenberg Press Limited, Malta

Contents

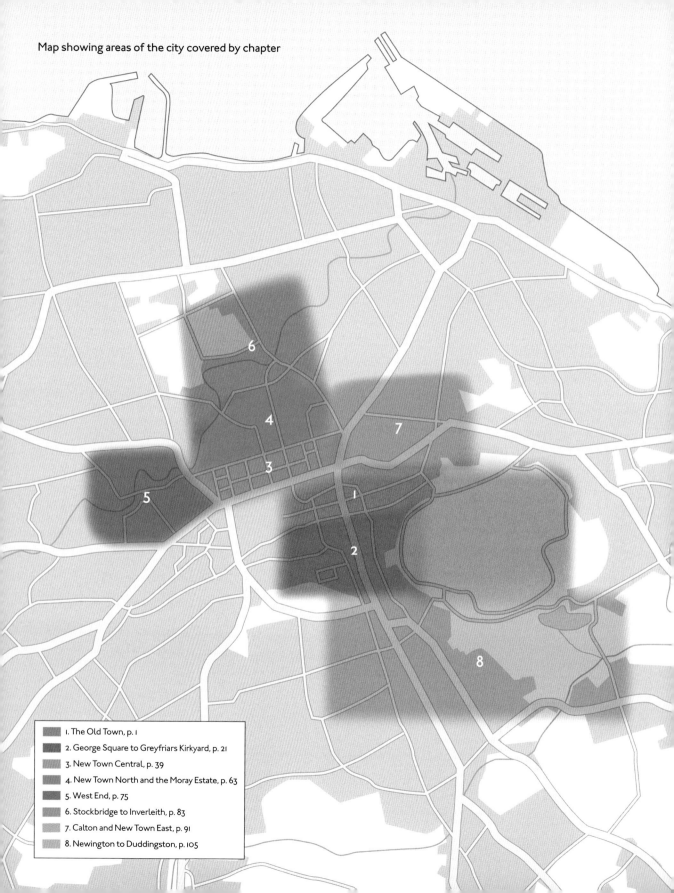

Map showing areas of the city covered by chapter

Introduction

Edinburgh has history written all over its Janus face. On one side, looking back in time, is a medieval city crowned by a castle that was built on rock over 350 million years old. On the other stands the 18th-century New Town, begun in 1767 as part of a vision to create an enlightened metropolis and European city of culture. Together they form one of the most spectacular cityscapes in the world.

How did this Enlightenment Edinburgh evolve? Who were the movers and shakers? Where did they meet, live, work and debate the great political, intellectual and physical challenges of the long 18th century? This little volume is an introduction to Enlightenment Edinburgh for the curious traveller.

After the Union with England in 1707, politicians and the gentry would take the high road from Edinburgh to London. The court and its entourage had left a century earlier after the Union of the Crowns in 1603. The result was a serious political and social vacuum in the capital. Thus began the long 18th century of rebellion, revolution and Enlightenment.

The Enlightenment was a cultural pan-European phenomenon marked by remarkable changes in law, philosophy, science, literature, the arts, engineering and architecture. The Age of Enlightenment went hand in hand with an Age of Improvement. For centuries Scotland had kept close cultural and political links with mainland Europe and this continued with Francis Hutcheson, David Hume, Adam Smith and Adam Ferguson being part of a community of European Enlightenment scholars that included Diderot, Goethe, Montesquieu and Voltaire. In Scotland, the most literate nation in Europe by 1750, the Enlightenment was driven forward by the urban intelligentsia of

'It is for those who inherit the achievement of Edinburgh's classical age to understand it, to adapt it, to use it and to enjoy it.'

A.J. Youngson,
The Making of Classical Edinburgh

*'Let rivers, hills, let woods and
    plains,
Let morning dews, let winds and
    rains,
United join to aid my woe,
And loudly mourn my
    overthrow.—
For Arthur's Ov'n and Edinburgh
    Cross,
Have, by new schemers, got a toss;
We, heels o'er head, are tumbled
    down,
The modern taste is London town.'*

Claudero (James Wilson), from The last
Speech and dying words of the CROSS of
Edinburgh, which was hanged, drawn and
quartered, on Monday the 15th of March
1756, for the horrid crime of being an
Incumbrance to the Street

*'Matters have considerably changed
by the great extension of
Edinburgh; both to the south and
north, coffee houses and booksellers'
shops are now dispersed in many
places; and literary men are not
now to be found at the Cross in
change hours, as formerly.'*

Robert Kerr,
Memoirs of William Smellie (1811)

Aberdeen, Edinburgh and Glasgow. Edinburgh, however, was the beating heart of the Enlightenment in Scotland. The intellectual courage and prowess of its philosophers along with the vision of its civic leaders created a new post-Union metropolis that put the city on the world stage.

In 1746 the Town Council of Edinburgh acknowledged the political reality of Hanoverian victory and Jacobite defeat at Culloden by sending the Duke of Cumberland the Freedom of the City of Edinburgh in a gold casket. In this post-Union, post-Culloden era, the city's greatest civic leader, Lord Provost George Drummond, pursued his vision to give Edinburgh a new urban identity and a new status as a great European city of culture. He started with new public buildings, the first being the Royal Infirmary (William Adam, 1738), the second the Royal Exchange (John Adam, 1753–61). In March 1756, the Cross of Edinburgh, for centuries the historic centre of civic life, was 'hanged drawn and quartered . . . for the horrid crime of being an incumbrance to the Street'. The creation of Enlightenment Edinburgh had begun.

By the 1750s, Edinburgh was physically bursting out of its medieval boundaries. The population had tripled to some 60,000 since the Union and would exceed 100,000 by the end of the century. Old Town citizens lived vertically and communally, muddied and muddled in high tenements 'where the toe of the peasant touched the heel of the courtier'. While Mylne's Court (1690), James's Court (c.1725) and Chessel's Court (c.1745) opened up some parts of the Old Town, most citizens lived 'cheek by jowl' in an Old Town that had the appearance of a medieval Manhattan. Social networks were created in the convivial atmosphere of the taverns, coffee houses, and masonic lodges. Here the serious business of drink and debate nurtured a cross-fertilisation of ideas across all classes. Conversation reigned supreme and conversations, then as now, would change the world.

The first exodus from the medieval confines of the Old Town was to the south in the 1760s with the building of George Square. The boldest leap, however, was northwards beyond the Castle and the Nor' Loch. Published in 1752 the *Proposals for carrying out certain Public Works in the City of Edinburgh* became the 'enlightened blueprint' for the greatest urban regeneration project of the century. It proclaimed that 'so necessary and so considerable an improvement of the capital cannot fail to have the greatest influence on the general prosperity of the nation'. It was time for a new rational urban order set in a rolling landscape of new ideas and opportunities.

Fifteen years later saw the 1767 *Act for extending the Royalty of the*

City and the adoption of James Craig's amended 1766 grid plan for the New Town. Deserting the sordid and overcrowded 'vertical' streets of the Old Town, the Edinburgh elite headed for champagne and chandeliers in the New Town. By the 1790s the social watershed was in full flood.

Traditional Scottish vernacular styles were abandoned as the New Town became a showcase for some of the finest civic and commercial monuments of the neo-classical revival in Europe. Robert Adam's rigid and clean-cut Palladian style was the preferred choice for the new 'gentleman architect' and 'builder architect' until the 19th century. Thereafter the 'professional architects' such as William Henry Playfair raised the Hellenic torch of the Greek revival to make Edinburgh, not only intellectually, but architecturally the 'Athens of the North'.

In defining the period known as the Scottish Enlightenment, some scholars have limited it to the era of Hutcheson, Hume and Smith while others extend its influence and impact through to the later generations of Dugald Stewart, Francis Jeffrey and Sir Walter Scott. This guide to the people and places of Enlightenment Edinburgh extends its reach towards 1850 to include the later generation of practical intellectuals in science, architecture and engineering who consolidated the legacy of the Enlightenment as a basis for the modern age. Leith is not part of this guide as it deserves a volume in its own right.

The city has been divided into sections with each section having a map showing the streets and significant locations mentioned in the text. A map of the whole city, showing the various areas covered in each chapter, can be found on p.vi. This is a personal selection of what merits attention in Enlightenment Edinburgh. All opinions and deviations in objectivity or accuracy are my own. A list of titles for further reading and research is given at the end of the main text.

There are no designated walking routes, so that readers can plan their own route through different parts of the city. 'All truly great thoughts are conceived by walking', observed Friedrich Nietzsche, and walking was a way of life for many of our great city's Enlightenment figures. For those who enjoy walking, it is still the best way to get closer to the history of the city and its people. Whilst this volume is for the curious traveller, it may also remind the citizens of Edinburgh that there is much to see and explore beyond their own neighbourhoods.

Explore. Discover. Enjoy Enlightenment Edinburgh.

Sheila Szatkowski
May 2017

'Piled deep and massy, close and high, mine own romantic town!'

Sir Walter Scott, *Marmion*

In Edinburgh, the access to men of parts is not only easy, but the conversation and the communication of their knowledge are at once imparted to intelligent strangers with the utmost liberality. The philosophers of Scotland have no nostrums. They tell what they know, and deliver their sentiments without disguise or reserve.'

Amyat, the King's Chemist, to William Smellie, printer in Edinburgh

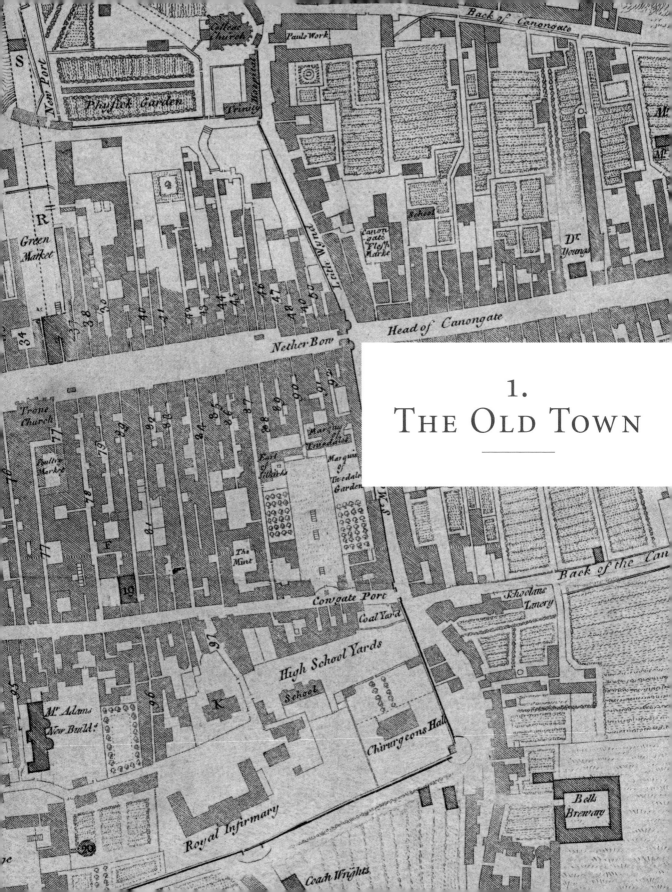

1.
THE OLD TOWN

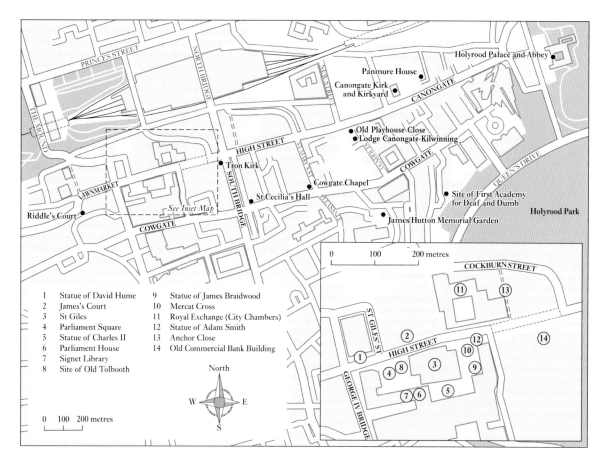

1 Statue of David Hume   **9** Statue of James Braidwood
2 James's Court   **10** Mercat Cross
3 St Giles   **11** Royal Exchange (City Chambers)
4 Parliament Square   **12** Statue of Adam Smith
5 Statue of Charles II   **13** Anchor Close
6 Parliament House   **14** Old Commercial Bank Building
7 Signet Library
8 Site of Old Tolbooth

Around St Giles and Parliament Square

'About seven months ago I got a house of my own, and completed a regular family, consisting of a head, viz. Myself, and two inferior members – a maid and a cat.'

David Hume, in a letter to John Clephane, 5 January 1753, on his home in Riddle's Court

'Reason is, and ought only to be the slave of the passions, and can never pretend to any other office than to serve and obey them.'

David Hume, *A Treatise of Human Nature*

Presiding over the main crossing of the Royal Mile at Bank Street is the **STATUE OF DAVID HUME** (1711–66), a one-man academy of arts and humanities and the last of the great empiricists. A most apt inscription to this great figure of Enlightenment Edinburgh can be found on the rear of the plinth: Philosopher and Historian. Scot and European. Man of the Enlightenment.

Close by in Lawnmarket are the sites of Hume's former homes in **RIDDLE'S COURT** and **JAMES'S COURT**. After moving to the New Town in 1771 with his sister Katharine and highly inquisitive companion, Foxey the Pomeranian, Hume rented out his home in James's Court to James Boswell, biographer of the great critic, writer and lexicographer Samuel Johnson. Boswell's supper guests during his time in James's Court included the famous Corsican patriot Pasquale Paoli and Johnson himself. South of the High Street is the old Parliament Close, now

Parliament Square, site of the original Advocates Library where Hume was Keeper from 1752 to 1757, a post he described with tongue firmly in cheek as the 'very pinnacle of human grandeur and felicity'. The Advocates Library was located 'in a series of lofty rooms under the Parliament House' and according to the printer William Smellie, 'to this noble collection, joined to the generosity of its proprietors, Scotland, for these hundred years past, has been much indebted for the many productions of genius and learning, which have enabled her sons within that period, to make such a distinguished figure in almost every department of science'.

St Giles

When the Scottish Act of Settlement of 1690 established a reformed Presbyterian Church as the national Church of Scotland after 50 years

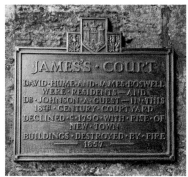

Top: Statue of David Hume by Alexander Stoddart.

Above: Plaque at the entrance to James's Court, Lawnmarket.

David Hume

An historian, philosopher and essayist, Hume in his *Treatise on Human Nature* (1739) proposed that the study of the science of human nature, based upon observation and experience, should underpin all study of moral philosophy, religion and politics. His other philosophical works, *An Enquiry Concerning Human Understanding* (1748) and *An Enquiry Concerning the Principles of Morals* (1751) brought him fame and extensive travel throughout Europe but it was his *History of England* (1754–62) which brought him fortune. As late as 1773, his publisher, William Strahan, failed to persuade him to write more, with Hume declaring, 'I must decline not only this offer, but all others of a literary nature for four reasons:

because I'm too old, too fat, too lazy, and too rich.'

Hume's unorthodox views on religion denied him academic posts in Edinburgh (1745) and Glasgow (1757). A bon vivant, he was an active member of many societies, joint Secretary of the Philosophical Society (f.1731) in the1750s and a founder of the Select Society (p.5). Founded in 1754, the Select Society was an elite debating club dedicated to 'the pursuit of philosophical enquiry and the improvement of the members in the art of speaking'. To ensure his name was pronounced correctly beyond Scotland, he styled himself Hume instead of Home from 1734, and in 1752 he also produced a list of Scotticisms or Scots usages to be avoided in all correspondence and publications.

'His manner of delivery was not equal to the matter of his discourses. It was stiff, formal and not altogether free from affectation.'

Thomas Somerville of Hugh Blair

Hugh Blair (1718–1800), cleric and author.

of bitter religious conflict, **ST GILES** became the Mother Kirk of Presbyterianism. Controversy and divisions persisted, however, culminating in the Great Disruption of 1843 which split the Church, but from the mid-18th century, the Kirk in Edinburgh was dominated by the Moderate clergy. Their leader was the Rev. William Robertson, and along with Hugh Blair, Adam Ferguson, Alexander Webster and Alexander 'Jupiter' Carlyle, they comprised a highly educated, influential and sociable group of reverend polymaths. The most sought-after pulpit in Edinburgh was the High Kirk of St Giles, and its most eminent preacher was Hugh Blair, minister from 1758 to 1777.

Robert Chambers recalled the High Kirk as having 'a sort of dignified aristocratic character . . . frequented only by sound church-and-state men, who did not care so much for the sermon, as for the gratification of sitting in the same place with his Majesty's Lords of Council and Session, and the Magistrates of Edinburgh, and who desired to be thought men of sufficient liberality and taste to appreciate the prelections of Blair'. In 1762 Blair became the first Regius Professor of Rhetoric and Belles Lettres at the University of Edinburgh in what would become the first Department of English in the world. As a young man he had heard Adam Smith's lectures on Belles Lettres at Edinburgh. Later Blair's *Sermons* and his *Lectures on Rhetoric and Belles Lettres*, running to numerous editions worldwide, made him a significant figure in the history of rhetoric. He was an admirer of the works of Robert Burns and promoted the authenticity of the poems of Ossian,

The Select Society

The clergy were well represented in Edinburgh clubs and societies, including the elite Select Society. Its members met weekly at the old Advocates Library in Parliament Square and debated topics such as divorce by mutual consent, slavery and export duties. Clerics conversed with philosophers such as David Hume and Adam Smith, liberal lawyers such as Lord Kames and William Johnstone (later Sir William Pulteney, friend and patron of the architect Robert Adam), medical luminaries such as John Hope and Alexander Monro, Primus, and artists such as Allan Ramsay. Henry Cockburn described such societies as 'powerfully productive of thought, of talent and even of modesty'.

In 1755 the Select Society extended its reach by setting up the Edinburgh Society for the Encouragement of Arts, Sciences, Manufactures and Agriculture 'TO ENCOURAGE genius, to reward industry, to cultivate the arts of peace, and objects deserving the attention of public-spirited persons'. As well as debating issues in trade, agriculture and the arts, the society also awarded premiums or prizes for 'superior merit or industry', thus acknowledging the combined power of intellect and enterprise.

Left to right: Henry Home, Lord Kames, judge and philosopher; Hugh Arnot, author, *The History of Edinburgh* (1779); James Burnett, Lord Monboddo, judge and philosopher by John Kay (1784). Kames and Monboddo were both members of the Select Society.

which many, including Dr Johnson, believed to be forgeries by the poet James Macpherson.

Another well-known member of the moderate clergy was John Home, friend and relative of Hume 'the Infidel', so called by James Boswell. Home was author of *Douglas*, the most famous play of the Scottish Enlightenment. Staged in the Canongate Theatre (p. 15) in 1756, it was lauded by colleagues and reputedly one spectator shouted out on opening night: 'Whaur's yer Wullie Shakespeare noo?' Considered scandalous by evangelicals in the Church of Scotland, *Douglas* prompted essays by clerics Adam Ferguson and John Witherspoon on the moral worth of theatre.

'No man ever did a designed injury to another, but at the same time he did a greater to himself.'

Lord Kames

Top: East side of Parliament Close c.1795 with statue of Charles II.

Above: Interior of Parliament House, home of the Scottish Parliament, 1637–1707.

Parliament Square (formerly Parliament Close)

After 1707 the legal profession became the superior social and intellectual elite of the city. Parliament House, emptied of politicians since the Union of Parliaments, soon filled up with 'men of the long robe'. Outside in Parliament Close, goldsmiths, clockmakers and booksellers continued to trade in full view of the lead **STATUE OF CHARLES II**. John's Coffee House in the Close was a favourite of magistrates, town councillors and young advocates. The final item on many legal fee notes was often the tavern bill, and in Parliament House many would 'turn fidgety about the hour of noon' waiting on the chimes of St Giles to announce the Old Town tradition of a daily meridian dram.

PARLIAMENT HOUSE is still part of the Scottish Courts and is accessible on weekdays when the courts are in session. Among the portraits and statues of 18th-century legal worthies on view in Parliament House are Henry Dundas, 1st Viscount Melville by Sir Francis Chantrey (1818); Robert Dundas, 2nd Viscount Melville by Sir Francis Chantrey (1824); Lord Cockburn by William Brodie (1863); Lord Jeffrey by Sir John Steell (1855); Lord President Blair by Sir Francis Chantrey (1815); Henry Erskine by Peter Turnerelli (1811); and Sir Walter Scott by John Green-

Legal worthies

Best known for his *Elements of Criticism* (1762), Henry Home, Lord Kames (1696–1782), judge, philosopher and agriculturist, was a prolific writer, even dictating notes on his deathbed. Anxious friends were berated thus: 'Would you have me stay with my tongue in my cheek until death comes to fetch me?'

One of the most eccentric judges in the Scottish Court was James Burnett, Lord Monboddo (1714–99), who disagreed with Hume's philosophy and regularly sparred with Lord Kames. His six-volume *Of the Origin and Progress of Language* (1773–92) anticipated Darwin's theories but made him the butt of caricature on account of his theory of mankind shedding their primeval tails. His daughter, Elizabeth, was a celebrated Edinburgh beauty whose premature death from consumption prompted an elegy from Burns.

Infamous as 'the hanging judge', Robert McQueen, Lord Braxfield (1722–99), earned his reputation during the sedition trials. After the political upheavals of the French Revolution, liberal and democratic movements were set up across Britain. On 26 July 1792, a group of burgh reformers, religious dissenters and radical artisans set up the Scottish Society of the Friends of the People at a meeting in Fortune's Tavern in Old Stamp Office Close. Within a year many of these reformers were on trial for sedition.

In later years the courts saw the arrival of new faces: Sir Walter Scott, Francis Jeffrey, Henry Brougham and Henry Cockburn. It was a young Henry Cockburn who berated Robert Reid's classical scheme to reface the old Parliament House and adjacent buildings in 1808, lamenting 'the bright freestone and contemptible decorations that now disgrace us'. Cockburn deemed the town council 'omnipotent, corrupt, impenetrable' and was convinced 'that King Charles tried to spur his horse against the vandals when he saw the profanation begin. But there was then such utter absence of public spirit in Edinburgh that the building might have been painted scarlet without anyone objecting.'

shields (1835). The statue of Justice (1637) by Alexander Mylne can be seen on the east–west corridor beyond Parliament House. Part of the rubble back wall of the original 17th-century Parliament House (James Murray, 1630–40) can still be seen from George IV Bridge.

Above. The Court of Session, Second Division, March 1812.

'The inhabitants . . . who are acquainted with the English . . . endeavour to speak like them, especially the politer sort of people, and the Professors of the College, who, in their lectures, strive to shake off the Scotch pronunciation as much as possible.'

Edward Topham, in a letter to the Hon. Wilham S., Esq. on 6 December 1774

Above: interior detail, Signet Library.

Above right: interior, Signet Library.

Opposite top: Old Tolbooth, demolished 1817, with the west end of St Giles to the right.

Opposite bottom: James Braidwood (1800–1861). He died in the Great Tooley Street Fire in London.

Great cities of Enlightenment need great libraries, and Edinburgh is privileged to have outstanding collections and magnificent buildings to house them. Next door to Parliament House is the **SIGNET LIBRARY**, with an upper library described by George IV as 'the finest drawing room in Europe'. The cupola painting in the Upper Library (home of the Advocates Library in the 1820s) by Thomas Stothard depicts Apollo and the Muses and an eclectic mix of ancient and modern heroes, including Burns, Shakespeare, Homer, Milton, Virgil, Cicero, Demosthenes, Herodotus, Livy, Hume, Robertson, Gibbon, Newton, Bacon, Napier and Adam Smith. The Garnkirk Urn, which stands at the west

end of the room, was made by the Garnkirk Coal Company in Lanarkshire and given to the Society in 1842. The Lower Library (William Stark, 1812–18) was the original library of the Writers to the Signet, Scotland's senior solicitors.

By 1817 it seemed that the Old Town wanted no truck with medieval construction and so the great 'disencumberment' began, with the demolition of the **OLD TOLBOOTH** west of St Giles and the old shops – the Krames and Luckenbooths (locked booths) – on its east side. Traders such as William Auld and Thomas Reid, who had adjacent shops in Parliament Close, formed a new partnership and moved to 33 Princes Street to capitalise on New Town trade. St Giles was later subjected to 'sacrilegious misdeeds', according to some, or 'restoration' by others, when William Burn re-faced the Kirk in Cullalo stone in the late 1820s.

The High Street to South Bridge

Standing to the east of St Giles is the **STATUE OF JAMES BRAIDWOOD**, a practical and enlightened man, who set up the world's first municipal fire service in Edinburgh in response to the Great Fire of 15 November 1824. The fire started in the workshop of engraver James Kirkwood at the top of the Old Assembly Close, 'where a pot of linseed oil had been

*'The old provost, who danced to
    the whistle
Of that arch-politician, the
    Dean of the Thistle.'*

Lord Dreghorn describing the influence of
the Reverend Dr John Jardine on his father-
in-law, Lord Provost George Drummond

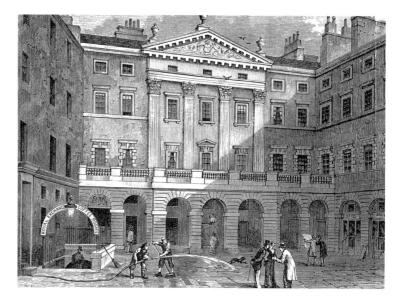

Above right: Royal Exchange and Royal
Exchange Coffee House (front, left), from
Thomas Shepherd's *Modern Athens* (1829).

Above: George Drummond (1688–1766), seven
times Lord Provost of Edinburgh. He 'stood in
the first rank of public characters in the
metropolis' (Thomas Somerville).

overheated, spilled and set fire to a stack of paper'. Most of the buildings
east of St Giles extending to the Tron Kirk and southward down
Fishmarket Close to the Cowgate were destroyed. James Nasmyth,
engineer, recalled that he and his father, the artist Alexander Nasmyth,
with 'a select party of the most distinguished inhabitants', watched the
fire from the tower of St Giles.

The **CROSS** or **MERCAT CROSS** had witnessed all civic life in the city
of Edinburgh: trading, public proclamations, celebrations, executions
and corporal punishment. The demolition in 1756 of this great symbol
of a medieval past marked the beginning of a new enlightened era for
the metropolis. In 1756 the Cross was positioned a few yards to the east,
still marked by an octagonal arrangement of cobble stones. In the late
19th century the Mercat Cross, incorporating some of the original
stones, was rebuilt on its present site east of St Giles.

In the post-Union, post-Culloden era, Lord Provost George
Drummond took forward his vision to give the city a new urban
identity and a new status as a great European city of culture. He started
with new public buildings, the first being the Royal Infirmary (William
Adam, 1738; pp. 30, 33) and second the **ROYAL EXCHANGE** (John Adam,
1753–61). Merchants shunned the Royal Exchange, preferring to trade
at the site of the old Mercat Cross as before, so in 1811 the town council
moved from the New Tolbooth behind St Giles to make the Royal
Exchange its new City Chambers. Along with the Kirk, law courts and
the university, civic government remained in the Old Town, as is the

case today. Only the physicians and archivists blazed a trail down the North Bridge to purpose-built homes in the New Town.

The **STATUE OF ADAM SMITH**, the first major monument in the world to honour the great philosopher and economist, looks downhill towards his former home in the Canongate. From 1777 until his death, Smith worked in the Royal Exchange as a Scottish Commissioner of Customs and Salt Duties for a salary of £600 per annum.

Sculptor Alexander Stoddart has given Smith the collar of Thomas Jefferson, the wig of George Washington and the robes of the University of Glasgow, perhaps to remind Edinburgh citizens that he never held an academic post in the capital. The plough represents old-style agrarian economics while the beehive is the symbol of industry on which Smith believed progress was based. Smith believed in an economic system based on individual self-interest. Using the example of a pin factory to show the advantage of the division of labour in increasing production, he proposed specialisation and free trade without oppressive tariffs. Such revolutionary views paved the way for the idea of the modern market economy that exists today. Although an academic post eluded Smith, his enlightened patron, Lord Kames, arranged for him to give lectures on Belles Lettres at Edinburgh University in 1748 which were so popular that he repeated them in the following two years. Like his great friend Hume, Smith travelled extensively in Europe and interacted with other intellectuals including Turgot, Quesnay, Necker and Voltaire. In London he met with leading politicians and no doubt frequented the British Coffee House in Cockspur Street, a popular meeting place for Scots in London.

Smith's *Theory of Moral Sentiments* appeared in 1759 (the same year as Voltaire's *Candide*, Alexander Gerard's *Essay on Taste* and Edmund Burke's second edition of *A Philosophical Enquiry into the Origins of our Ideas of the Sublime and Beautiful*, with a new tract on 'Taste'). After many years working as a 'solitary philosopher', Smith's landmark thesis, *An Inquiry into the Nature and Causes of the Wealth of Nations* was published by W. Strahan (Strachan in Scotland) and T. Cadell in London on 9 March 1776, a few months before the American Declaration of Independence.

Although Smith and Hume published their works in London, it did not stop Edinburgh becoming a major centre for publishing in the 18th and early 19th centuries, where literature was considered 'the staple produce of the metropolis'. Print culture was key to the spread of ideas amongst a highly literate populace. Near the site of the Cross, publisher William Creech hosted his morning levees for the literati. In earlier

Statue of Adam Smith (1723–90) by Alexander Stoddart.

'*It is not from the benevolence of the butcher, the brewer, or the baker, that we expect our dinner, but from their regard to their own interest. We address ourselves, not to their humanity but to their self-love, and never talk to them of our own necessities but of their advantages.*'

Adam Smith, *The Wealth of Nations* (1776)

'*Hatred and anger are the greatest poison to the happiness of a good mind.*'

Adam Smith, *The Theory of Moral Sentiments* (1759)

Scots and slavery

Adam Smith supported the fight for independence in the American colonies. He deemed slavery uneconomic and immoral, and along with other Enlightenment luminaries questioned the meaning of freedom in society and its economic impact. For David Hume, it was 'cruel and oppressive', while William Robertson preached against slavery and sent his sermons to William Wilberforce. In February 1788 William Creech, as Secretary of the Chamber of Commerce, prepared one of the earliest petitions to parliament to ban slavery, while the Rev. Robert Walker, subject of *The Skating Minister* in the National Gallery of Scotland, urged the Edinburgh presbytery to follow suit. The Abolitionist Committee in Edinburgh, led by retired judge Francis Garden, Lord Gardenstone, was one of the most active bodies in Britain.

But as Scots owned or managed one-third of Jamaican land under plantation in the late 18th century there were clearly others who condoned slavery. Robert Gordon, bookseller, 30 Parliament Close, advertised his 'full powers to conclude a bargain' for 'A BLACK BOY' in the *Caledonian Mercury* of 28 January 1769. After the Joseph Knight v John Wedderburn case in Edinburgh in 1778, it became illegal to own a slave in Scotland, prompting the *Caledonian Mercury* to announce that 'it must give a very high satisfaction to the inhabitants of this part of the united kingdom, that the freedom of negroes has received its first general determination in the Supreme Court of Scotland'.

years Allan Ramsay, author of *The Tea Table Miscellany* (1724) and *The Gentle Shepherd* (1725), had set up Britain's first circulating library nearby at the east end of the Luckenbooths. Walter Ruddiman of Forresters Wynd, was proprietor of the *Weekly Magazine*, a digest of news and reviews with a circulation of some 3,000 copies in the 1770s. In 1773 Ruddiman published *Poems* by Robert Fergusson, the Edinburgh bard much admired by Robert Burns.

Another enterprising publisher, Peter Williamson unveiled the first Edinburgh street directory in 1773, with an apology for omissions, citing that many had 'scruples of giving information, as they imagined it was for another purpose he was taking up their names'. Williamson also organised a system of penny postage for letters and parcels throughout the city and Leith.

Top: Commemorative medal issued for the unveiling of the Adam Smith statue in Edinburgh in 2008.

Above: William Creech (1745–1815), publisher and Lord Provost of Edinburgh.

Right: Medal celebrating the bicentenary of *Encyclopaedia Britannica*.

The most literary close in the Old Town must be **ANCHOR CLOSE**, where the *Encyclopaedia Britannica* started publication in 1768, written for the most part by William Smellie. It was an early form of 'cut and paste' composition, with Smellie admitting, 'I wrote most of it . . . and snipped out from books enough material for the printer. With pastepot and scissors I composed it!' His colleague Andrew Bell supplied 160 copperplate illustrations. Smellie was an accomplished antiquary and naturalist, receiving an enviable £1,000 advance from Charles Elliot for his *Philosophy of Natural History*. A keen golfer and member of the Burgess Golfing Society, he is famous for winning a bet to drive a ball from Parliament Square over the spire of St Giles.

Smellie printed the Edinburgh edition of Burns's *Poems* in 1787 and introduced the poet to the faithful and enthusiastic patrons of the Crochallan Fencibles at Douglas's Tavern in Anchor Close, a few steps away from his printing office. Another club favoured by the toping classes was the Cape Club (f.1764), whose members represented a cross-section from the trades, arts and professions, such as Robert Fergusson the poet, the infamous Deacon Brodie, believed by many to be the model for R.L. Stevenson's *The Strange Case of Dr Jekyll and Mr Hyde*, Smellie, Henry Raeburn, Henry Erskine and the antiquary David Herd.

A hidden treasure in New Assembly Close is the **OLD COMMERCIAL BANK BUILDING**, built in 1813–14 by James Gillespie Graham (p. 71). The Close took its name from the old Assembly Rooms that flourished there

Anchor Close from Cockburn Street.

John Kay (1742–1826), Paparazzo of Enlightenment Edinburgh

Few cities in the world have a social document to match Kay's *Portraits*, a remarkable collection of etchings by Edinburgh's self-taught miniaturist and etcher, John Kay. First published in 1837, the volumes contain over 250 etchings of characters from all walks of life who were part of Enlightenment Edinburgh. Kay's etchings include the well-known or kenspeckle citizens of the city such as Adam Smith, but the real gems are his likenesses and caricatures of ordinary townsfolk, soldiers, visitors such as the balloonist Lunardi and infamous characters such as Deacon Brodie. A plaque at 227 High Street marks the house where Kay died in 1826, aged 84 years.

Above left: South Bridge from the Cowgate.

Above right: Old Commercial Bank Building in New Assembly Close, the site of the Assembly Rooms from 1766 to 1784. Novelist, playwright and poet Oliver Goldsmith attended assemblies in the Close and lamented that there was 'no more intercourse between the sexes than between two countries at war'.

Opposite top: Cowgate Chapel, now St Patrick's Roman Catholic Church.

Opposite middle: Plaque at the entrance of Panmure House.

'. . . . *for a long course of years his shop, during a part of the day, was the resort of most of the clergy of the city, of the professors of the University, and other public men and eminent authors; and his dwelling-house was equally frequented in the morning hours by many of the same characters, who met to discuss with him their literary projects.'*

Dugald Stewart, writing about William Creech, publisher

from 1766 to 1784 when public subscription allowed for a much grander edifice to be built in the fashionable New Town.

A tron was a public weigh-bridge. The Butter tron in the Lawnmarket was demolished in 1822 while the Salt tron stood near the present **TRON KIRK**. Begun in 1637, to a design by John Mylne, the Tron Kirk was truncated on the east, west and south sides in the late 1780s to allow the building of North Bridge, Hunter Square and **SOUTH BRIDGE**. Hunter Square and Blair Street were named after Lord Provost Sir James Hunter-Blair who rejected Robert Adam's ambitious plans for the new South Bridge development in favour of the more modest scheme of Robert Kay, James Brown and John Baxter Junior. The South Bridge, complete with 19 arches, opened to carriages less than three years after the foundation stone was laid on 1 August 1785 by Lord Haddo as masonic Grand Master of Scotland.

The Cowgate, Canongate and Holyrood

One of the forgotten gems of Enlightenment Edinburgh is **ST CECILIA'S HALL** (Robert Mylne, 1761) at the bottom of Niddry Street in the Cowgate. The oldest purpose-built concert hall in Scotland, and the second oldest in Britain (after the Holywell Music Room in Oxford), it has been thoughtfully restored to its former glory by the University of Edinburgh and houses the renowned Russell Collection of Early Keyboard Instruments. Here it is possible to hear 18th-century music in an 18th-century concert hall played on 18th-century instruments. Modelled on the Opera House at Parma and built for the Edinburgh Musical (or Harmonical) Society, the walls 'vibrated to the strains of the Messiah' and to the voices of Domenico Corri and the castrato Senesino. In 1787, the building of the new South Bridge made access to the hall difficult, and the Society's meetings moved to St John's Lodge in the Canongate. The Hall later served as Freemasons' Hall from 1809 to 1844.

Close by is the old **COWGATE CHAPEL**, now St Patrick's Roman Catholic Church. When it first opened, the Cowgate Chapel (John Baxter Jr, 1774) was the most prominent of the 'qualified' Episcopalian chapels. A qualified chapel was an Episcopal congregation that worshipped liturgically while accepting the Hanoverian king and thereby 'qualified' under the Scottish Episcopalians Act of 1711, for exemption from the penal laws against the Episcopal Church in Scotland. The 18th-century historian Hugo Arnot wrote of the Cowgate Chapel that it was 'a mark of increasing moderation and liberality among the people. Not many years ago that form of worship in all its ceremonies would not have been tolerated.'

Despite the exodus of nobility after the Union of the Crowns in 1603, the **CANONGATE** area, being less compacted than the High Street and Lawnmarket, remained home to many residents of note in the 18th century. A walk from the Cross to the Canongate in the early 1780s would have presented many interesting encounters with older Enlightenment worthies who seemed content to linger in the Old Town. Adam Smith would walk up from his home at **PANMURE HOUSE** (129 Canongate) to his office at the Royal Exchange. Lord Monboddo would amble home, often sending his wig ahead of him in a sedan chair in case it got damp in the haar (sea mist). James Boswell went regularly to New Street to visit Lord Kames in his dying days, recording on 3 December 1782 that he was 'weaker and somewhat fretful. Found Mr Craig, the architect showing him plans of the New Town, which he looked at with a keen eye.'

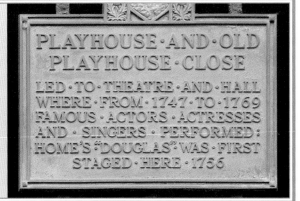

Old Playhouse Close

The first performance of John Home's *Douglas* ran at the Canongate Theatre in 1756. Originally founded in 1748 as the Canongate Concert Hall by the eminent engraver Richard Cooper the Elder, the playhouse was known for performances of radical works and was the first purpose-built theatre in Scotland. The building was later incorporated into Lodge Canongate Kilwinning. It was the same Richard Cooper who founded the Edinburgh School of St Luke in 1729, the earliest academy of artists in Scotland.

Robert Fergusson (1750–74), Edinburgh poet, described by Robert Burns as 'my elder brother in the muse'.

No sculptured marble here,
   nor pompous lay,
No storied urn nor animated bust;
This simple stone directs pale
   Scotia's way,
To pour her sorrows o'er the
   Poet's dust.

Inscription by Robert Burns on the gravestone of Robert Fergusson

In the evening there would have been others heading downhill to a learned supper at Lord Monboddo's home in St John Street or perhaps joining their fellow Masons at **LODGE CANONGATE KILWINNING**. Many Enlightenment figures were members of this lodge: Henry Mackenzie, author of *The Man of Feeling*, Henry Erskine, Dugald Stewart, William Creech, William Smellie, James Boswell, Alexander Nasmyth, James Gregory MD, the Earl of Buchan, the banker Sir William Forbes and Robert Burns, who was admitted to the Lodge in February 1787.

Besides the Lodge, Burns had other connections in the Canongate. His friend, John Campbell, Precentor at the **CANONGATE KIRK** (James Smith, 1688) introduced him to the Kirk Baillies whom Burns persuaded to erect a monument to Edinburgh's own bard, Robert Fergusson (1750–74). Fergusson also has a statue on the pavement outside the Kirk.

Walking in a clockwise direction from the front of the kirk, the first notable grave on the west wall of the kirkyard is that of the visionary Lord Provost George Drummond. Turning left to the south-west corner allows a view of the graves of Adam Smith, philosopher and economist, and physician James Gregory, who believed that 'the best physician is one who can distinguish what he can do from what he cannot do'. Gregory gave his name to the famous laxative and tonic, Gregory's Powder. A few yards to the north is Fergusson's grave and further downhill is the large mausoleum to the moral philosopher Dugald Stewart. On the east side of the kirkyard can be found the final resting place of Sir Walter Scott's great friends, the publishers James and John Ballantyne, as well as Charles Alston, King's Botanist at Holyrood Palace. Two eminent academics lie close together near the exit: the Rev. John Walker, Professor of Natural History at Edinburgh and Keeper of the Natural History Museum 1779–1803, and the eminent surgeon Benjamin Bell, who published *A System of Surgery* in 1783, the first comprehensive surgical textbook in the English language. Canongate Kirkyard is also the resting place of Robert Burns's Clarinda (Agnes M'Lehose), whose unconsummated affair with the poet inspired him to write 'Ae Fond Kiss', one of his most popular poems.

No British monarch set foot in **HOLYROOD PALACE** during the Scottish Enlightenment. However foreign royals and aristocratic exiles found it a convenient residence. Determined to have her son educated in Edinburgh, the Russian Princess Ekaterina Dashkova arrived in 1776 and lived for six years in the palace. Twice weekly, she hosted visits from William Robertson, Adam Smith, Hugh Blair and Adam Ferguson, describing them as 'generally esteemed for their intelligence, intellectual

---

A Canongate wedding

A spring wedding in the Canongate Kirk on 1 March 1752 saw Allan Ramsay (1713–84), the great Scottish portraitist, marry Margaret Lindsay, against the wishes of her stern father, Sir Alexander Lindsay, 3rd Baronet of Evelix. Margaret's brother, Sir John Lindsay, also defied convention by fathering an illegitimate mixed-race daughter, Dido Elizabeth Belle, later Murray. Dido was brought up by the family of Lord Mansfield, the Lord Chief Justice, who made several landmark rulings on slavery that were among Britain's first steps towards abolition.

Born in Edinburgh, the son of Allan Ramsay (1686–1758), poet, Ramsay Junior was an artist of European significance who truly engaged with his European contemporaries. At home he refused a knighthood and rejected the Royal Academy. He was a competent linguist, speaking fluent French to Voltaire and Diderot, and German to Queen Charlotte. He helped design his father's house, 'Guse-pye' in Ramsay Garden, near Edinburgh Castle (p. 57) and in later life, after an injury to his right arm, took up writing, with tracts on politics, archaeology and a 'Dialogue on Taste'.

In 1745 Ramsay was summoned to Holyrood Palace to paint a half-length portrait of Prince Charles Edward Stuart (Bonnie Prince Charlie) soon after his victory at the Battle of Prestonpans. Perhaps in anticipation of further victories the prince is depicted in a velvet robe fringed with ermine and the blue riband and star of the Order of the Garter. Engravings of the portrait were widely circulated to promote the Jacobite cause. The portrait is now part of the collection of the National Galleries of Scotland.

distinction, and moral qualities'. On her return to Russia she became the first woman to lead a national science academy, as director of the Russian Imperial Academy of Sciences in St Petersburg. In this role she awarded William Robertson, Principal of the University of Edinburgh, the honorary degree of Doctor of Sacred Theology.

Thousands of debtors claimed sanctuary within the bounds of **HOLYROOD ABBEY**, including Thomas DeQuincey and Charles-Philippe, Comte d'Artois, younger brother of the French king Louis XVI. Defeated, exiled and unable to pay his soldiers, he arrived at

Above left. The Palace of Holyroodhouse from Thomas Shepherd's *Modern Athens* (1829).

Above right. Grave memorial in Canongate Kirkyard for Agnes M'Lehose, known as 'Clarinda', for whom Burns wrote 'Ae Fond Kiss'.

Holyrood in 1796, having been granted refuge by the British government. He returned a second time as the exiled Charles X in 1830 and stayed for two years. In 1829 Felix Mendelssohn drew inspiration from a visit to Holyrood Abbey, writing, 'I believe I found today in that old chapel the beginning of my Scottish Symphony.'

An unsung hero of 18th-century Edinburgh is Thomas Braidwood (1715–1806), an early pioneer of sign language and founder of the **FIRST ACADEMY FOR THE DEAF AND DUMB IN BRITAIN** opened in 1760 and located to the south of the Cowgate. In 2015, soon after the passing of the landmark British Sign Language (Scotland) Act at the Scottish Parliament, a plaque was mounted on a portion of the academy wall that is still visible on Dumbiedykes Road.

A memorial garden at St John's Hill marks the **SITE OF THE HOME OF JAMES HUTTON**, pioneer of modern geology. He died there on 26 March

Opposite top left: Lord Adam Gordon, Governor of Edinburgh Castle and the Count d'Artois, afterwards Charles X (1796), by John Kay.

Opposite top right: James Hutton (1726–97) father of modern geology, by John Kay (1787).

Opposite bottom: Plaque to commemorate the first Academy for the Deaf and Dumb in Britain.

Left: James Hutton and Joseph Black, 'Philosophers', by John Kay (1787).

1797 and was buried in Greyfriars Kirkyard. Too ill to deliver his first lecture to the Royal Society of Edinburgh in 1785, James Hutton asked his great friend and colleague Joseph Black to read out his paper. The content of this and Hutton's second paper was revolutionary, proposing that the process of rock formation and erosion was a very slow cyclic one, meaning that the earth was much older than the 6,000 years or so suggested by the Creationists. Hutton proclaimed that there was 'no vestige of a beginning and no prospect of an end'. A similar theory had been postulated 20 years earlier by Mikhail Lomonosov (1711–65), the Russian father of geology and co-founder of Moscow State University, in a paper entitled 'On the Strata of the Earth' (1763), but Hutton delivered the evidence. His research in **HOLYROOD PARK**, the discovery of the geological 'unconformities' at Siccar Point in Berwickshire, and other revelations shared with fellow explorers John Playfair, Sir James Hall and John Clerk of Eldin, proved his theories and confirmed him as the true father of modern geology.

'The result, therefore, of this physical enquiry is that we find no vestige of a beginning, no prospect of an end.'

James Hutton, *The Theory of the Earth*

'Upon the whole, Chymistry is as yet but an opening science, closely connected with the usefull and ornamental arts, and worthy the attention of the liberal mind.'

Joseph Black

The Clerks of Penicuik

The Clerks of Penicuik as a family exercised a major influence on the cultural history and intellectual life of Scotland over five generations. A gifted artist, John Clerk of Eldin (1728–1812) hailed from the fourth generation. He produced the drawings for James Hutton's *Theory of the Earth* (Hutton dedicated the first copy to him), and in the 1790s completed his famous *Essay on Naval Tactics* that notably changed the Admiralty's strategy on fighting sea battles. Such tactics would prove decisive in the years leading up to Nelson's victory in 1805 at Trafalgar. Clerk of Eldin married Susanna, daughter of the architect William Adam. He was the great-great uncle of the eminent scientist James Clerk Maxwell.

'You have great Advantages in going to study at Edinburgh at this Time, where there happens to be collected a Set of as truly great Men Professors of the several Branches of Knowledge, as have ever appeared in any Age or Country.'

Benjamin Franklin in a letter to Benjamin Rush
and Jonathan Potts, December 20, 1766

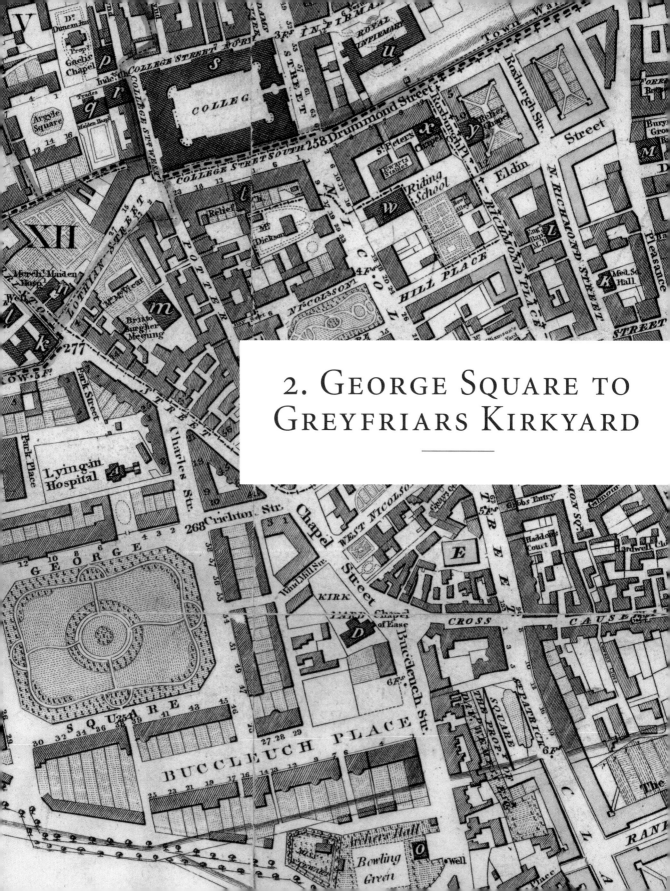

2. George Square to Greyfriars Kirkyard

*'Edinburgh is considerably
extended on the south side, where
there are divers little elegant
squares built in the English manner;
and the citizens have planned
some improvements in the north,
which when put in execution,
will add greatly to the beauty
and convenience of this capital.'*

Tobias Smollet, *Humphry Clinker*, 1771

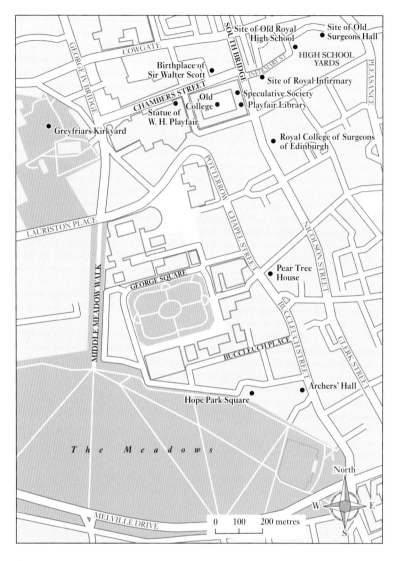

*'As the ground declines towards the
southern side of this square . . . it is
one of the most cheerful residences
in Edinburgh, on account of its
rural prospects . . .'*

Robert Forsyth, on George Square, 1805

George Square and The Meadows

In 1761 the town council turned down the offer of land in the policies
of Ross House between the Potterrow and the Meadows. The young
speculative James Brown bought the 26 acres for £1,200 and developed
GEORGE SQUARE, the first spacious square outside of the medieval city.
It was a bold and risky move but an elite of legal and aristocratic buyers
craving a private home became enduring residents. Located just south
of the Potterrow, no new bridge or access route was required, thus
making George Square (named George after James Brown's brother)

seem much closer to the Old Town than the fledgling New Town on the distant ridge to the north. The few 18th-century buildings to survive today are on the west and east sides of the Square, overlooked by one of the key examples of Scottish Modernism, the David Hume Tower of Edinburgh University.

Nearby, at **2 BUCCLEUCH PLACE** and later at 4 George Square, lived the Rev. Dr John Jamieson whose two great loves were his wife and his dictionary. *Jamieson's Etymological Dictionary of the Scottish Language* appeared in two volumes in 1808, with a further two volumes in 1825. In the 1808 edition the 'S' section alone contained 2,200 entries, mostly supported by written citations based on Jamieson's research. The current *Scottish National Dictionary* includes extensive material from Jamieson's volumes.

A new locale required a dance hall, so in 1785 the Assembly Rooms opened in the rear wing of Nos 14–16 Buccleuch Place. Here, Lady Don of George Square and her partner in etiquette, Mrs Lochead of Inverleith, enforced strict ballroom discipline on both the 'hooped beauties in the minuet' and hopeful partners, such as Henry Cockburn and Sir Walter Scott.

Set close to a Venetian window on the first floor of No. 18 Buccleuch

Above: George Square, west side. Sir Walter Scott lived at No. 25.

Below: John Jamieson (1759–1838), compiler of the first historical *Dictionary of the Scots Language* (1808, 1825).

Residents of George Square

No. 29, with its round-arched door, was the home of James Brown. The redoubtable Lady Don lived at No. 53 and is often cited as the last person in Edinburgh to own a private sedan chair. Sir Walter Scott's family moved from College Wynd to No. 25 in 1774, and the young Scott lived here until his marriage in 1797. John Bradfute, of Bell and Bradfute, Booksellers, lived at No. 22, and it was here that a young Jane Welsh would visit Mr Bradfute's niece, Miss Eliza Stodart, and in the same house enjoy the attentions of Thomas Carlyle. On the east side lived Lord Chief Baron Robert Dundas (1758–1819) at No. 57, with his next-door neighbour at No. 56 being Robert Blair (1741–1811), Lord President of the Court of Session. The gentility of the square was given a severe jolt during the king's birthday celebrations in June 1792 when a large pugnacious mob burnt an effigy of Henry Dundas (1742–1811), 'the uncrowned king of Scotland', the most powerful politician in Scotland of his day, outside the Lord Chief Baron's house. Henry Dundas died at No. 57 in May 1811.

On the north side of the square (now demolished) was the home of Lord Braxfield. Braxfield's doorway survives in a house in the Blacket estate. Braxfield was the last of the bench to use pure Scotch idiom and was not afraid of his Scotticisms. During the highly charged atmosphere of the sedition trials in the 1790s, Braxfield would walk from court to his home in George Square, alone and without protection. He died there on 30 May 1799.

Above: Robert McQueen, Lord Braxfield (1722–99), lived at 13 George Square, north side (now demolished).

Left: Henry Dundas, 1st Viscount Melville, and Robert Dundas of Arniston, Lord Chief Baron of the Court of Exchequer.

Place, an unassuming plaque marks the birthplace in 1802 of the most respected and influential British magazine of the 19th century – *The Edinburgh Review*. Founded by members of the Select Society (p. 5) in 1755, with contributions from Adam Smith, Hugh Blair and William Robertson, the first *Edinburgh Review* offered 'frank criticism of native publications' but closed after two issues. The editors of the 1802 *Review* were a new generation, nurtured in debate and intellectual discovery at the Speculative Society (p. 29) and at the lectures of Dugald Stewart, successor to Adam Ferguson in the Chair of Moral Philosophy at Edinburgh. In this new *Review* Francis Jeffrey, Sydney Smith, Francis Horner and Henry Brougham edified a 'British' public that was as keen on debate, discussion and intellectual discovery as they were themselves. Between the blue-and-yellow covers, much of the content of the *Review* promoted Whig politics and soon there were rival magazines, such as the *Quarterly* in London (1809), to which Walter Scott was a contributor, and in 1817 the combative *Blackwood's Edinburgh Magazine*, also known as *Maga*. Thomas Carlyle, a contributor, described the *Review* as 'a kind of Delphic Oracle' and there was no doubt as to its impact on the reputations and readership for other authors' work. Byron's 'English Bards and Scotch Reviewers' was a piqued response to the *Review*'s critique of his first published work, *Hours of Idleness*.

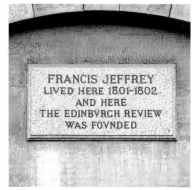

Above: 18 Buccleuch Place, home of Francis Jeffrey and *The Edinburgh Review*.

Below: Hope Park Square.

One of the earliest improvements on the south side was the laying out of **THE MEADOWS** (known as Hope Park) on the newly drained Boroughloch in the 1730s by Sir Thomas Hope of Rankeillor. Sir Thomas was a founder member and first President of the Society of Improvers in the Knowledge of Agriculture in Scotland (1723), the first of many patriotic agricultural improvement societies in Europe. Hope's scheme consisted of open parkland and tree-lined walks such as **MIDDLE MEADOW WALK** (1743). Henry Cockburn remarked: 'Under these trees walked, and talked, and meditated, all our literary and scientific and many of our legal worthies.' **No. 6 HOPE PARK SQUARE** was originally built by Sir Thomas Hope as Hope House, a private dwelling now part of Hope Park Square.

Nearby in Buccleuch Street is **ARCHERS' HALL** built in 1766 for the Royal Company of Archers, the Sovereign's Body Guard in Scotland. A plate on the founding stone of Archers' Hall declared: 'Nulla Caledoniam gens unquam impune lacesset' (None whosoever provoke Caledonia go unpunished), a defiant statement for a club of 18th-century archers whose members included Sir Walter Scott, Sir Henry Raeburn and Robert Burns.

Burns and the South Side

Robert Burns knew this area well. He spent three weeks in 1787 at the home of William Nicol, 'that obstinate son of Latin Prose', who lived in St Patrick Street, now part of Buccleuch Street. He also called on Thomas Blacklock (1721–91) at **PEAR TREE HOUSE** (1749) at the corner of Chapel Street and West Nicolson Street, now a public house. Thomas Blacklock, 'the Blind Poet', hosted many great literary figures, including David Hume (who gave an annuity to Blacklock), Benjamin Franklin and Dr Johnson. Hume described him as 'a very elegant genius, of a modest backward temper, accompanied with that delicate pride which so naturally attends virtue in distress'. Blacklock certainly helped to alleviate the economic distress of Robert Burns, whom he persuaded in 1786 to abandon his plans for Jamaica and to pursue a second edition of his poems in Edinburgh. Burns had 1,500 subscribers to his Edinburgh edition.

South Bridge and Old College

Robert Kay (1740–1818), architect of the South Bridge.

An expensive grand plan featuring a level roadway from the North Bridge to Nicolson Street set on high arches and lined with colonnaded porticoes and shops comprised Robert Adam's design submission for the **SOUTH BRIDGE**. In the end, Lord Provost James Hunter-Blair opted for the affordable but inferior option offered by Robert Kay and others, and the South Bridge opened in 1788. However, a bigger prize awaited Adam the following year, when he was appointed to build a new college for his old alma mater.

Adam's design for the new college, now known as **OLD COLLEGE**, comprised two courtyards, one to serve as professorial residences and the other as the main teaching block, with a library and museum. Adam

Left: Old College, exterior, early 19th century.

Below left: Old College quadrangle in the 21st century.

Scotland's universities

Before the Reformation, Scotland had three universities while England had two. By the 18th century, there were five north of the border: St Andrews (1411), Glasgow (1451), King's College, Aberdeen (1495), Marischal College, Aberdeen (1593) and Edinburgh (1583). England had two, Oxford and Cambridge, albeit with many constituent colleges. By 1750 the effects of the 1696 Education Act for the 'Settling of Schools' in every parish led to Scotland becoming the most literate nation in Europe. At the same time the University of Edinburgh had achieved a worldwide reputation for specialist teaching and academic excellence, especially in medicine, and most classes were taught in English. By the 1780s the army of intellectual soldiers who had stormed the bastions of intellectual thought and philosophy at Edinburgh University were demanding new quarters worthy of their achievements and status.

was present on 16 November 1789 when the founding stone was laid by Lord Napier, Grand Master Mason, in the presence of Lord Provost Elder, Principal William Robertson and a crowd of some 30,000, which included the pupils of the nearby High School, who had been given a half-day holiday to attend the spectacle.

The scheme was halted in 1792 on account of war in Europe and the death of both architect and his cousin, Principal William Robertson. Only the east front and the north-west corner of Adam's plan were built. The magnificent vaulted entrance was framed by six monolithic pillars of Craigleith sandstone (1791), the largest single

Playfair Library, Old College, one of the finest
neoclassical interiors in Britain.

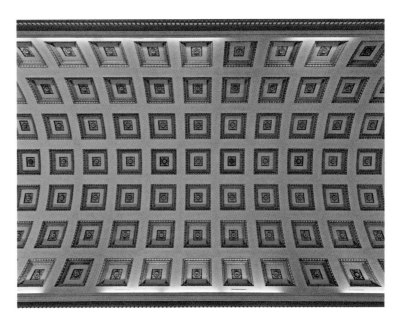

pieces ever cut from Craigleith Quarry (p. 85). Robert's Reid plan to complete the project in 1810 did not go ahead. Finally, in 1816 William Henry (W.H.) Playfair, a young 26-year-old protégé of architect William Stark, entered and won the competition for the completion of Robert Adam's university building. It was the start of a long and productive career for Playfair, and Old College represents one of his major contributions to classical Edinburgh. The magnificent barrel-vaulted ceiling of the **PLAYFAIR LIBRARY** remains one of the finest neo-classical interiors in Britain.

The buildings on the south side were built in 1826–7, with Playfair's final contribution in 1840 being the iron gates at the South Bridge entrance. The dome, a familiar feature of Edinburgh's skyline, was added by Robert Rowand Anderson in 1887 and the lawn in the quadrangle was a very late addition of 2011, funded by an anonymous £1 million gift. Old College is also home to the **SPECULATIVE SOCIETY**. Founded in 1764 'for improvement in Literary Composition and Public Speaking,' the Speculative Society still meets in its rooms in Old

'. . . the Speculative completed what the Academical had begun; and together they did me more good than all the rest of my education.'

Henry Cockburn, a member of the Academical and the Speculative debating societies

Meeting room of the Speculative Society (founded 1764), Old College.

Above: Statue of William Henry Playfair in Chambers Street, by Alexander Stoddart.

Below: Ornament from William Adam's Royal Infirmary, now sited at the Drummond Street entrance to High School Yards.

College. As a young student, William Creech, the publisher, was its first president and later members included David Hume, John Clerk of Eldin, Dugald Stewart, Francis Jeffrey and Sir Walter Scott.

It is hard to find a place in the city without a view to a building or monument designed by W.H. Playfair. He was a perfectionist, always practising what he preached, namely that 'Nothing good in Architecture can be affected without a monstrous expenditure of patience and India Rubber'. The new **STATUE OF W.H. PLAYFAIR** by Alexander Stoddart outside the National Museum of Scotland in Chambers Street is a welcome commemoration of one of the city's most famous architects. Facing Playfair is the statue of William Chambers (1800–83), publisher, former Lord Provost and civic heir to Lord Provost George Drummond.

William Playfair did not have to go far for his next grand design, a new home for the **ROYAL COLLEGE OF SURGEONS OF EDINBURGH** just south of Old College. The chosen site was that of the old Riding Academy in Nicolson Street, built in 1763 to the design of Robert Adam but put up for auction on account of debt. Playfair rose to the challenge of the relatively small site with a T-plan temple fronted by a large-scale entrance featuring six free-standing Ionic columns across the entire front elevation. The building was completed in 1832. Old College and the Royal College of Surgeons were sited on the main carriage route from the south to the Athens of the North. Surgeons' Hall Museum on Nicolson Street, set up as a medical teaching resource, expanded in the early 19th century to include the remarkable collections of Sir Charles Bell and John Barclay. It is now open to the public with extensive displays on the history of medicine in the 18th and 19th centuries.

High School Yards to Greyfriars

The new medical school of 1726 required a hospital for clinical teaching. Subsequently a small hospital opened in Robertson's Close in 1729 and was deemed worthy of a Royal Charter in 1736. Such royal status warranted a grander edifice. William Adam, father of the Adam dynasty, was appointed architect of a new 228-bed **ROYAL INFIRMARY OF EDINBURGH** begun in 1738 on the south side of Infirmary Street near the present site of Dovecot Studios. Public subscriptions included monies from Archibald Kerr, whose Jamaican estate, with around 40 slaves, produced enough revenue to allow some £200 to be paid annually to the hospital. Sadly, Adam's infirmary, the first great public building beyond the medieval Old Town, was demolished in the 1880s

From Tounis College to renowned university

During the 18th century the Tounis College of Edinburgh, founded in 1583, became the beating heart of the Enlightenment in Scotland. The College was controlled by the Town Council with teaching by Regents who taught all subjects to the same students throughout their degree course. William Carstares, Principal from 1703 to 1715, persuaded the Council to replace these Regents with Professorships in individual subjects. Later, William Robertson, Principal from 1762 to 1793, consolidated the university's international reputation with many key appointments including Hugh Blair to the Chair of Rhetoric and Belles Lettres and Dugald Stewart as successor to Adam Ferguson in the Chair of Moral Philosophy.

But it was the establishment of the Medical Faculty in 1726, modelled on the school in Leiden and achieved through the joint efforts of medic John Monro (1670–1740) and Lord Provost George Drummond, that transformed the Tounis College into a world-class university. In the 1760s over half of the university's 600 or so students were enrolled in the Medical Faculty. Many were from America, such as Benjamin Rush, William Shippen, John Morgan and Adam Kuhn, who established the medical school at Philadelphia in 1765, and Samuel Bard, who in 1767 founded the first medical school at King's College, New York, now Columbia University. The Monro family provided the greatest of the medical dynasties in Edinburgh. John Monro, Deacon of the Incorporation of Surgeons, ensured his son Alexander Monro Primus was appointed Professor of Anatomy in 1720.

Monro Primus and Secundus were outstanding teachers, but the lectures of Monro Tertius wearied the likes of Charles Darwin. A more enthusiastic audience attended his dissection in Old College of the infamous murderer William Burke, hanged outside St Giles on 28 January 1829.

Other prominent medical names include Andrew Duncan, Professor of the Institutes of Medicine (Physiology), who set up the first public dispensary in Richmond Street and the lunatic asylum, and William Cullen, Professor of the Institutes of Medicine (Physiology) and of the Practice of Medicine, famous for keeping copies of all his correspondence, created with a copying machine invented by his friend James Watt.

Professors charged fees for their classes but as part of the Tounis College they were bound by loyalties to the city as well as to the university and so opened their lectures to polite society, including women. James Boswell attended a course of lectures on chemistry with Joseph Black in 1775. The ladies seemed to favour Dr T.C. Hope, with Henry Cockburn writing to a friend, that Hope 'receives 300 of them by a back window, which he has converted into a door. Each of them brings a beau, and the ladies declare that there was never anything so delightful as these chemical flirtations.' Professor John Leslie resorted to desperate measures to compete for an audience, dying his hair in various vibrant shades to attract attention!

Left to right: William Robertson, Principal of Edinburgh University from 1762 to 1793; Alexander Monro Secundus (1733–1817) and Andrew Duncan (1744–1828), by John Kay.

Some noteworthy students of the 18th and early 19th centuries

Robert Adam (1728–92), architect

James Miranda Barry (c.1795–1865) (MD 1812) Inspector General of Military Hospitals. Recently identified as Margaret Ann Bulkley, thus the world's first female medical graduate

James Boswell (1740–95), biographer of Dr Samuel Johnson

Robert Brown (1773–1858), of Brownian motion fame

Thomas Carlyle (1795–1881), the 'Sage of Chelsea'

James Clerk Maxwell (1831-1879) Theoretical physicist

Charles Darwin (1809–82). Darwin's father, grandfather and uncle all studied medicine at the University of Edinburgh. Darwin left after two years, without graduating

Oliver Goldsmith (1728–74), novelist and playwright

David Hume (1711–76), historian and philosopher

James Hutton (1726–97), geologist

William Jardine (1784–1843), co-founder of Jardine, Matheson & Co. in 1832

James Lind (1716-1794), pioneer in the treatment of scurvy

W.H. Playfair (1790-1857), Architect

John Rennie (1761–1821), engineer (Kelso Bridge; Waterloo Bridge)

Peter Mark Roget (1779–1869), compiler of Roget's *Thesaurus*

Benjamin Rush (1746–1813), signatory of the American Declaration of Independence, 1776

Sir Walter Scott (1771–1832), novelist

Sir Robert Sibbald (1641–1722), physician, founder of the Royal College of Physicians of Edinburgh

John Witherspoon (1723–94), signatory of the American Declaration of Independence, 1776

Daniel Rutherford (1749–1819), chemist. Discovered nitrogen in 1772

Empty chairs

Neither David Hume nor Adam Smith ever held an academic post at Edinburgh University. Philosopher Francis Hutcheson, who taught Adam Smith at Glasgow University, declined a Chair in Philosophy in 1745 and actively blocked David Hume's application for the same post. In 1819, Charles Babbage failed to get a professorship in Mathematics, the preferred choice being William Wallace, a Scottish mathematician and astronomer who taught the Scottish mathematician and scientist Mary Somerville. Alumnus James Clerk Maxwell also failed to get a Chair in Natural Philosophy, but succeeded at King's College, London. His genius was finally acknowledged by his alma mater in 1870 with an honorary degree of Doctor of Law.

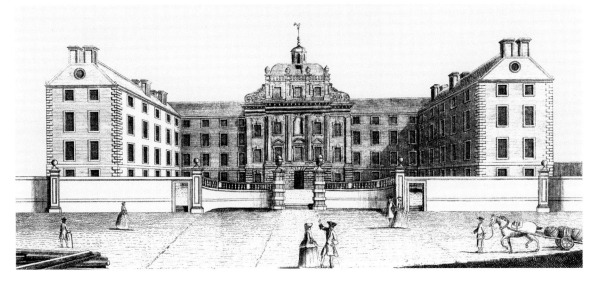

Royal Infirmary of Edinburgh, Infirmary Street, by William Adam (1738–42), demolished c.1882.

after a replacement was built in Lauriston Place.

The building of the new Royal High School on Regent Road (p. 100) and the Edinburgh Academy in the New Town (pp. 87–88) led to the **OLD ROYAL HIGH SCHOOL** being sold to the Royal Infirmary in 1829. Three years later it opened as a surgical hospital. Today it is the University's Centre for Carbon Innovation. Famous attendees of the Royal High School included George Drummond, James Lind, Henry Cockburn and Sir Walter Scott. Cockburn described the school as 'notorious for its severity and riotousness' but admired its worthy principal, Dr Alexander Adam. Adam, he remarked, was 'born to teach Latin, some Greek and all virtue'. Scott, another admirer, said of him: 'It was from this respectable man that I first learnt the value of knowledge.'

To the east of High School Yards, the **OLD SURGEONS' HALL** (1696–97) can still be seen in Old Surgeons' Square. The Incorporation of

'Perhaps there is at present no spot upon the earth where religion, science, and literature combine more to produce moral and intellectual pleasures than in the metropolis of Scotland.'

Benjamin Rush, Signatory, American Declaration of Independence, MD Edinburgh, 1768

'Medicine is taught in Edinburgh in greater perfection than in any other part of Europe.'

Benjamin Bell, surgeon (1749–1806)

Above: Old Royal High School, which became part of the Royal Infirmary in 1832.

Right: Old Surgeons' Hall (1697) in High School Yards.

Below: Plaque in Guthrie Street marking the birthplace of Sir Walter Scott.

Barber Surgeons was founded in 1505 and gained a Royal Charter in 1778. At Old Surgeons' Hall in 1702, the great physician Archibald Pitcairne presided over the first public dissection in Scotland of a human body. Visitors to Surgeons' Square in the early 19th century would have passed by the anatomy school of Robert Knox and the former home of the Royal Medical Society. Established in 1737, it is the only student medical society in Britain to hold a Royal Charter, awarded in 1778 by George III.

On the east wall of Guthrie Street, off Chambers Street, is a plaque marking the **BIRTHPLACE OF SIR WALTER SCOTT** in 1771. He was the son of Walter Scott, WS and Anne Rutherford, daughter of John Rutherford, Professor of Medicine at Edinburgh University. The family moved to 25 George Square in 1775.

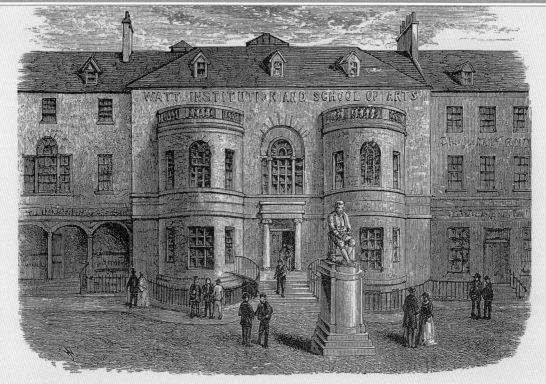

The beginnings of adult education

Education took a new direction in the early 19th century, with a focus on the practical application of knowledge and learning for the betterment of society. Edinburgh took the lead, with the founding of the first Mechanics Institute in Britain. With new advances in science and technology requiring workers with specific practical skills, Leonard Horner, with the co-operation of Professor James Pillans and Sir David Brewster, set up the School of Arts in 1821 'for the avowed purpose of enabling industrious tradesmen to become acquainted with the principles of mechanics, chemistry and other branches of science of practical application in their several trades'.

The School of Arts was first based at the Free-masons Hall in Niddry Street, then in Adam Square (demolished in 1869, along with Arygle Square and Brown Square, to make way for Chambers Street) as the Watt Institution and School of Arts. There anyone could have access to classes in chemistry, mechanics and natural philosophy, as well as geology, mechanical and architectural drawing, and even farriery. By 1833, a formal Diploma of Life Membership of the School of Arts was available on successful completion of a three-year course in mathematics, chemistry and physics. The school evolved to become Heriot-Watt University.

Above: The Watt Institution and School of Arts, demolished to make way for Chambers Street.

Right: James Watt (1736–1819), Scots inventor and industrialist.

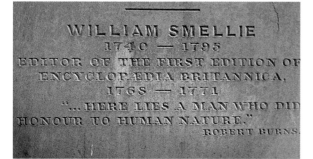

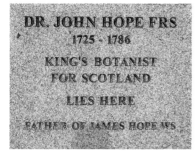

Above: Memorials in Greyfriars Kirkyard.

Opposite: The home of Joseph Black in Nicolson Street (now demolished).

Many of the great figures of the Scottish Enlightenment are buried in **GREYFRIARS KIRKYARD** – a large wooden display board at the entrance highlights noteworthy internments – but through oversight or some unexplained grudge against Aesculapius, there are no medical names listed.

On a cold December day at the close of the 18th century one of the great Enlightenment figures, Joseph Black, Professor of Chemistry, was laid to rest in Greyfriars Kirkyard. The Principal and the professors in their dark academic gowns, preceded by the mace, led the procession from the library of the college on South Bridge, with several hundred pensive students following close behind. The body of their esteemed colleague and teacher was brought down the steps of his home in Nicolson Street for its final journey through Chapel Street to Greyfriars, where it was laid to rest at the south-west corner and close to his great friend, James Hutton. Leaving the two great philosophers to continue their conversations in another world, the procession returned through Brown's Square and Argyll's Square (demolished in the 1860s to make way for Chambers Street) to the college. In a detailed will, Black requested that his white seal, set in gold, with a head of Plato, be given to the 3rd Earl of Hopetoun. The seal had been a gift to Black from the 2nd Earl, one of the first Governors of the Royal Infirmary of Edinburgh. Black's home, listed as **12 NICOLSON STREET** in the 1798–99 Edinburgh Street Directory, became the Royal Blind Asylum. Black was succeeded in the Chair of Chemistry by Thomas Charles Hope, son of John Hope, Professor of Botany and Regius Keeper of the Royal Botanic Garden of Edinburgh. Both professors are buried in Greyfriars.

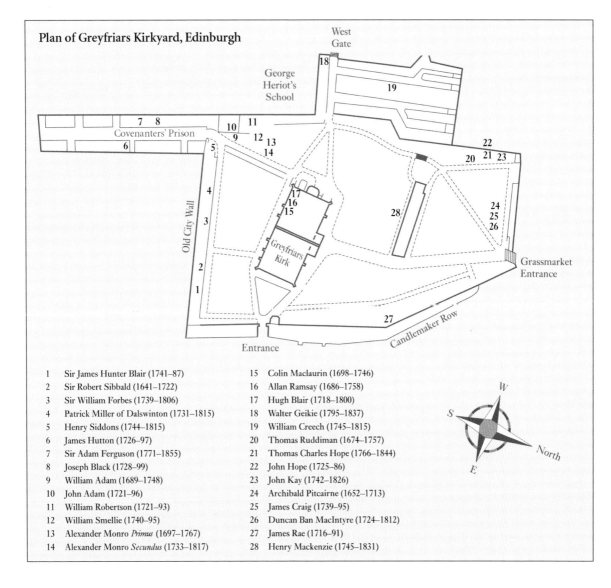

Plan of Greyfriars Kirkyard, Edinburgh

West Gate

George Heriot's School

Covenanters' Prison

Old City Wall

Greyfriars Kirk

Grassmarket Entrance

Candlemaker Row

Entrance

1	Sir James Hunter Blair (1741–87)	15	Colin Maclaurin (1698–1746)
2	Sir Robert Sibbald (1641–1722)	16	Allan Ramsay (1686–1758)
3	Sir William Forbes (1739–1806)	17	Hugh Blair (1718–1800)
4	Patrick Miller of Dalswinton (1731–1815)	18	Walter Geikie (1795–1837)
5	Henry Siddons (1744–1815)	19	William Creech (1745–1815)
6	James Hutton (1726–97)	20	Thomas Ruddiman (1674–1757)
7	Sir Adam Ferguson (1771–1855)	21	Thomas Charles Hope (1766–1844)
8	Joseph Black (1728–99)	22	John Hope (1725–86)
9	William Adam (1689–1748)	23	John Kay (1742–1826)
10	John Adam (1721–96)	24	Archibald Pitcairne (1652–1713)
11	William Robertson (1721–93)	25	James Craig (1739–95)
12	William Smellie (1740–95)	26	Duncan Ban MacIntyre (1724–1812)
13	Alexander Monro *Primus* (1697–1767)	27	James Rae (1716–91)
14	Alexander Monro *Secundus* (1733–1817)	28	Henry Mackenzie (1745–1831)

'Look at these fields … you, Mr Somerville, are a young man, and may probably live, though I will not, to see all these fields covered with houses, forming a splendid and magnificent city. To the accomplishment of this, nothing more is necessary than draining the North Loch, and providing proper access from the old town. I have never lost sight of this object since the year 1725, when I was first elected Provost.'

George Drummond to Thomas Somerville quoted in *My Own Life and Times 1741–1814*

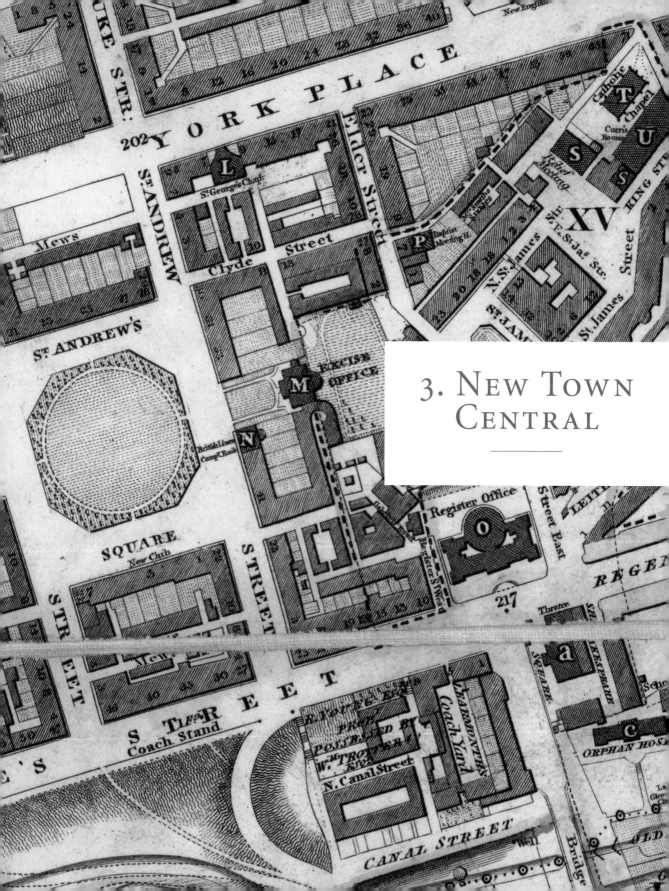

3. NEW TOWN CENTRAL

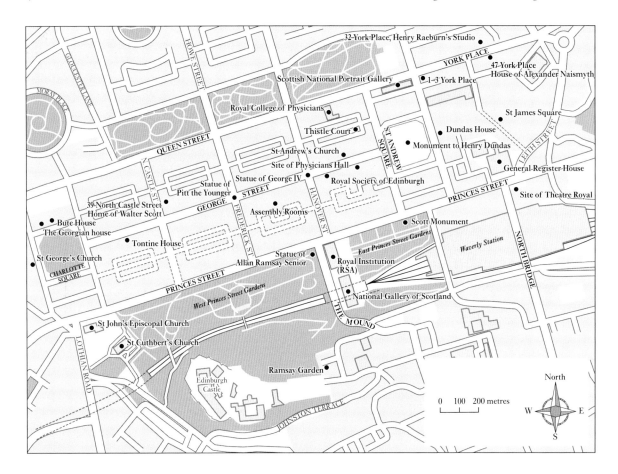

The Road to a New Town

'The addition of from 7 to 800 new dwelling houses to Edinburgh every year for some years past one would think must thro' time overstock the market and lower the rents, but this state of matters has not yet taken place.'

Anon., 1 March 1823, quoted in *Extracts from An Edinburgh Journal*, 1823–33

On 21 October 1763, a few months after the Treaty of Hubertusburg ended the Seven Years' War, Lord Provost Drummond laid the foundation stone of the new **NORTH BRIDGE**.

In 1767 the 'Act for the Extension of the Royalty' was passed and on 26 October that year James Craig laid the foundation stone of **THISTLE COURT**, and one John Young was given a premium of £20 to build the first house in the New Town. James Craig's plan was based on a symmetrical grid centred on the axis of George Street. Two grand squares were set at either end of George Street with two terraces, Queen Street facing north to the Firth of Forth and Princes Street facing south towards the Old Town.

The North or Nor' Loch in the valley below was drained and by 1772 the new bridge became the main route north from the Old Town. (The

present North Bridge dates from 1896.) On St Andrew's Day, 1775, James Boswell, as Master of the Canongate Kilwinning Lodge, led the procession of the Free Masons from the Parliament House over the North Bridge to the new Theatre Royal in Shakespeare Square. 'It had an excellent effect upon the New Bridge,' he noted, 'while the flambeaux blazed in a luminous train.'

This New Town was to become the physical embodiment of a new, enlightened Edinburgh. The old Scots vernacular style of the Old Town would gave way to a new architectural language that was classical. It would create order and civility but at the same time social and cultural segregation. The story of Scotland's capital was to become a tale of two cities.

Little remains of **ST JAMES SQUARE** (1773), designed by James Craig and built on Clelands Land, north of Leith Street. David Martin, who painted many Enlightenment figures, such as Joseph Black and David Hume, lived at 4 St James Square and died there in 1797. His portrait of one of Edinburgh's most famous visitors, Benjamin Franklin, hangs in the White House, Washington DC. In 1826 John J. Audubon took a short walk from his lodgings in George Street to St James Square to meet with W.H. Lizars, the artist who engraved the first plates for his

Top: View of the North Bridge and Old Town, late 18th century.

Above: Thistle Court, the first house in the New Town and not typical of the architectural style that came to define the area.

New styles for a New Town

While many houses were 'in the manner of the English' – that is, one house inhabited by one family top to bottom – others were built to look like a single house, but in fact comprised grand apartments. Familiar Old Town features such as coats of arms, gargoyles and marriage lintels gave way to formal classical details, fanlights and transoms. The hackney carriage replaced the sedan chair of the Old Town. Windows were bigger, sometimes bricked up in the hope of window tax being rescinded or set back as 'blind' recesses for aesthetic reasons. Houses were connected to form terraces; ironwork railings and balconies appeared; new furniture and wallpapers were chosen from catalogues and pattern books. 'I own, therefore I am' appeared to be the byword for the residents of the booming New Town.

Politeness represented the new social manners of Georgian society. Drawing, music and French lessons were the preferred accomplishments for young ladies. Elegance and refinement permeated all aspects of social intercourse, as conversations moved from a rowdy tavern of strangers to an elegant drawing room of polite society.

Conscious of these new social mores, and with an eye to business, Robert and James Adam advised in their *Works in Architecture* (1773) that: 'The eating rooms are considered as the apartments of conversation, in which we are to pass a great part of our time. This renders it desirable to have them fitted up with elegance and splendour, but in a style different from that of other apartments.'

St James Square: only the west side remains today.

'. . . all these splendid buildings are of trivial import compared with the mass of intellect and science which had taken root and had been nurtured and grown up to such a height as to rival, and perhaps to outstrip, every other city in the world.'

Thomas Bewick (1753–1828) of his second visit to Edinburgh in 1823

Birds of America. Audubon spent several weeks in Edinburgh, meeting Sir Walter Scott, Sir James Hall, Robert Knox and others, as well as taking in a performance of *Rob Roy*, where he noted that the 'ladies of the second class go to the pit, the superior classes to the boxes, and those of neither, unfit to be classified, way above'.

Designed by Robert Adam, with additional work by Robert Reid in the 1820s, **GENERAL REGISTER HOUSE** (1774) was the first purpose-built public record repository in Britain. James Boswell watched Lord Frederick Campbell lay the foundation stone, while his architect friend 'Bob' Adam looked on. Boswell 'was very angry that there was no procession, no show or solemnity of any kind on such an occasion'. Despite a grant of £12,000 from forfeited Jacobite estates, lack of funds delayed completion until 1789, prompting the publisher William Creech to describe the empty shell as 'the most magnificent pigeon-house in Europe'. James Tytler stored his Grand Edinburgh Fire Balloon in the building in 1784 before demonstrating the first British manned balloon flight in the Comely Gardens, near Holyrood, later that year.

Inside, the stunning top-lit domed rotunda inspired by the Pantheon in Rome, retains Adam's decorative scheme with plasterwork by local craftsman Thomas Clayton. The cast-iron railing around the gallery was made by the Carron Company to Adam's design. The statue of King George III (1787) inside the building was commissioned by Lord Frederick Campbell from his niece, Mrs Anne Seymour Damer. It appears amateurish in comparison to Ceracchi's fine sculpture of said Mrs Damer in the British Museum.

Top: Register House (1774), by Robert Adam.

Above: View to the Castle from Register House.

'The Gentlemen who have subscribed . . . for the Edinburgh Fire Balloon, are requested to attend to the Register Office, New Town . . . in order to see it filled, and to give their opinion as to what is further necessary to be done before its removal from the place, where it now is.'

Edinburgh Evening Courant, 17 July 1784

'... *for genius, worth and for agreeable manners, I know none whom I should rank above the friend we have lost* ...'

William Robertson, writing to Andrew Dalziel of the demise of Robert Adam in 1792

The exterior screen wall (1788) of Register House once extended to the edge of the main street, complete with iron railings, gates, lamp standards and lamp irons made to Adam's designs, again by the Carron Company. This screen wall was moved back to its present position in the late 19th century and replica lamps have replaced the originals. The clock of 1790 in the turret of the south-east tower of Register House and the wind vane on the south-west tower were supplied by Benjamin Vulliamy. Vulliamy, of Pall Mall in London, supplied the Regulator Clock for the King's Observatory at Kew, which served as the Prime Meridian from 1780 until the Greenwich Royal Observatory took over in 1884. Adam's 1785 plan for an elegant terrace of ten houses east of General Register House at Leith Street was never realised.

St Andrew Square

The grandest house in the New Town, **DUNDAS HOUSE**, at 36 St Andrew Square was designed by Sir William Chambers in 1771 for Sir Lawrence Dundas of Kerse. It was a Palladian villa modelled on Marble Hill in Twickenham. Known as 'the Forager' on account of his lucrative contracts to supply the Hanoverian army, Dundas thwarted Craig's plan for a large church at both ends of the central axis of George Street. Dundas had power and influence and wealth. He was a major landowner with plantations in Dominica and Grenada, as well as being MP for Edinburgh from 1768 to 1780, Governor of the Royal Bank of

Below: William Burn's monument to Henry Dundas, St Andrew Square from Thomas Shepherd's *Modern Athens* (1829).

Right: Dundas House, 36 St Andrew Square.

Scotland, and a major shareholder in the East India Company.

Noteworthy above the main door is a Royal Coat of Arms, added after Dundas House became the Principal Office of the Excise in 1794. It is unusual in that it retains the fleur-de-lys device representing the British monarch's claim to France. After the Treaty of Amiens in 1801, which temporarily suspended hostilities between Britain and France, this device was removed from the Royal Coat of Arms. The Royal Bank bought the building in 1825 for £35,300 (about £2.5 million in today's money) and it became the new headquarters for the bank. Today it is much altered inside, except for the original dining room upstairs on the north side. The railings, gates and the porch with its ornamental lamps date from the late 1820s.

The statue in the garden court of John, 4th Earl of Hopetoun, 'in Roman costume leaning on a pawing charger', was commissioned for Charlotte Square by the town council but then deemed unsuitable. As the Earl had been Governor of the Royal Bank from 1820 to 1823 it was agreed in 1834 to have it outside Dundas House.

Another Dundas dominates St Andrew Square, with William Burn's **MONUMENT TO HENRY DUNDAS**, 1st Viscount Melville, also known as Harry the Ninth on account of his political power in Scotland in the 1790s. Henry Cockburn condemned the town council for being 'omnipotent, corrupt, impenetrable ... no variety of opinion disturbed its equanimity, for the pleasure of Dundas was the sole rule for every one of them'. The poet Robert Fergusson had also lampooned his civic leaders many years earlier with the lines:

> For politics are a' their mark,
> Bribes latent, and corruption dark.

Few of the original houses remain in St Andrew Square. **No. 35 ST ANDREW SQUARE** (1769), next door to the Harvey Nichols department store, was designed by Robert Adam and is the oldest building in the square. It was the former Douglas Hotel, patronised by Sir Walter Scott, Queen Victoria and Empress Eugénie, wife of Napoleon III.

On the north side, a plaque at **23 ST ANDREW SQUARE** marks the birthplace of one of the great sons of Enlightenment Edinburgh, the abolitionist and reforming Lord Chancellor, Henry, Lord Brougham. An active promotor of the Reform Bill of 1832, this lad o' pairts also designed the Brougham carriage, founded the resort of Cannes and in 1826 helped to set up University College, London, a non-denominational college that followed the curriculum and academic style of the

---

New residents in St Andrew Square

By the early 1770s the exodus from the Old Town had begun. Some were heading south to George Square but those that set up home in St Andrew Square at this time included David Hume; Sir Andrew Crosbie, advocate; Sir George Chalmers; William Pulteney, advocate; Sir Adam Ferguson, advocate; the Earl of Buchan, founder of the Society of Antiquaries; and the Dowager Countess of Leven.

Benjamin Franklin stayed as a guest of Hume in his new home in South St David Street (now demolished) for almost a month on his last visit to Edinburgh in 1771. One of the last great Enlightenment suppers was held at Hume's home when he entertained Adam Smith, Joseph Black, John Home, Hugh Blair and Adam Ferguson shortly before his death. That same day, Franklin was at the Continental Congress to approve the final wording of an historic document on liberty and equality, the American Declaration of Independence. It was 4 July 1776.

University of Edinburgh. The square was still residential in the 1820s, with James Hamilton Senior, Professor of Midwifery, living at No. 23, his son James Hamilton Junior at No. 22 and Robert Nasmyth, surgeon and dentist, at No. 21.

Many Enlightenment figures were keen to embark on commercial ventures. In 1812 the social reformers Professor John Playfair and Robert Owen, publisher Archibald Constable and others met at the Royal Exchange Coffee House to consider 'a general fund for securing provisions to widows, sisters and other females'. In 1815 this became the Scottish Widows' Fund and Life Assurance Society, Scotland's first mutual life office. It was headquartered from the 1820s to 1970 in St Andrew Square. Sir Walter Scott was chairman of the Edinburgh Gas Light Company. George Drummond was a founding director of the Royal Bank of Scotland in 1727 and was the first to receive a loan (£1,000) from the bank. New Town residents were not as 'clubbable' as those in the Old Town, but the New Club was set up in the New Town in 1787 as a private members' club by members of the Caledonian Hunt. In 1809 the club met at 3 St Andrew Square before removing to Princes Street in 1837.

George Street

George Street was the central axis of Craig's plan. However it did not have the sunny aspect or dramatic views that led to Princes Street becoming the main thoroughfare of the New Town.

With Dundas House occupying the prime site on the square, **ST ANDREW'S CHURCH** (1781–4), the first church in the New Town – now known as St Andrew's and St George's – was built in George Street. It was designed by Major Andrew Fraser, who lived close by at No. 5 George Street in a house later occupied by the publisher William Creech. The 168-foot (51-metre) spire (William Sibbald, 1787) made the church the tallest building and thus a prominent landmark in the New Town. Inside the church many original 18th-century features remain including the Adam-style ceiling and several box pews. The 18th-century pulpit stood much higher in 1784 ensuring that the minister was placed 'six feet above contradiction'. It was here in 1843 that the Rev. Thomas Chalmers led the great Disruption of the Church of Scotland, the schism of the established Church which led to the founding of the Free Church of Scotland.

Across the street, with its six grand Corinthian pillars, the Dome Bar & Grill occupies the premises of the former Commercial Bank designed in 1845 by David Rhind. The Bank was built on the **SITE OF PHYSICIANS' HALL** designed by the New Town architect James Craig for the Royal College of Physicians. On 27 November 1775, William Cullen, President of the College, laid the foundation stone in the presence of all the Fellows, but mounting debts in the 1840s forced its sale to the

Opposite top: The south-east corner of St. Andrew Square from Thomas Shepherd's *Modern Athens* (1829).

Opposite bottom: Henry, Lord Brougham (1778–1868), who was born at 23 St Andrew Square.

Above: St Andrew's and St George's Church, at the east end of George Street.

Left: Physicians' Hall, George Street, by James Craig, demolished 1844 (from Thomas Shepherd's *Modern Athens*, 1829).

'To His Grace, Henry, Duke of Buccleuch, these tales, which in elder times have celebrated the prowess, and cheered the halls, of his gallant ancestors, are respectfully inscribed by His Grace's much obliged and most humble servant, Walter Scott.'

Scott's Dedication of the *Minstrelsy of the Scottish Border* to the 3rd Duke of Buccleuch, first President of the Royal Society of Edinburgh

Above left: Statue of George IV by Sir Francis Chantrey, funded by public subscription.

Above right: The present home of the Royal Society of Edinburgh.

'I felt that I had seen, not one, but two cities, a city of the past and of the present set down side by side, as if for the purposes of comparison, with a picturesque valley drawn like a deep score between them, to mark off the line of division.'

Hugh Miller, on his first view of Edinburgh in 1824

Commercial Bank. After renting premises at 119 George Street from 1843 to 1846 the College moved to its present home in Queen Street.

James Ferrier, friend of Sir Walter Scott, and his wife Helen Coutts Ferrier lived at **25 GEORGE STREET**, a house which stood near the northeast corner of Hanover Street. Their daughter, the author Susan Ferrier, met Burns here. She was also well acquainted with the Misses Edmonstone of Duntreath next door, whom she immortalised in her novel *Marriage* (1818), as Aunts Jacky, Grizzy and Nicky.

One of the greatest institutions of the Enlightenment period was **THE ROYAL SOCIETY OF EDINBURGH** (RSE). In 1782 William Robertson, Principal of the University, proposed to his colleagues in the Philosophical Society, 'a New Society, on a more extended plan, and after the model of some of the foreign Academies, which have for their object the cultivation of every branch of science, erudition and taste'. The first meeting was held in the Old Library of the university on 23 June 1783 and in due course all members of the Philosophical Society became Fellows of the new RSE. One member, the Earl of Buchan, opted out to establish the Society of Antiquaries which for a time met at his home at 1 St Andrew Street on the south-east corner of St Andrew Square.

Though based in Edinburgh, the RSE was not parochial, inviting academics from beyond Scotland, such as Benjamin Franklin, to become Fellows. Meetings were held at the Physicians' Hall, 14 George Street, from 1807 to 1810, until the Society bought 42 George Street, which then became its home until 1826. The RSE then moved to the Royal Institution on Princes Street (now the Royal Scottish Academy) before settling into its present home at 22–26 George Street.

The visit of George IV in 1822 sent the capital into a frenzy, though some, such as Thomas Carlyle, decided to get out of town to escape the 'efflorescence of flunkeyisms'. The **STATUE OF GEORGE IV** (Chantrey, 1831) at the junction of Hanover Street and George Street commemorates the visit.

The great and good turned out in their finery to see the king at a ball at **THE ASSEMBLY ROOMS**, at a banquet at the Parliament Hall in the Old Town and at a stage adaptation by Isaac Pocock of Sir Walter Scott's *Rob Roy* at the Theatre Royal. Artists including Alexander Nasmyth, Alexander Carse, David Wilkie and J.M.W. Turner rolled up like 18th-century *paparazzi* to commit the event to canvas. Wilkie's fine portrait of the king resplendent in Highland garb hangs in the dining room of Holyrood Palace.

A royal visit

Stage-managed by Sir Walter Scott, the visit began with the king, George IV, stepping off the *Royal George* (escorted into port by two steam vessels, the *James Watt* and the *Comet*) at Leith on Scott's 51st birthday. Steamboats expedited the arrival of spectators coming via the old Queensferry Crossing while the new canal barges brought onlookers from the west. The king was accompanied by the newly elected Home Secretary Sir Robert Peel, the Duke of Wellington and Sir William Curtis MP, Lord Mayor of London. The city was awash with uniforms and tartan. Colonel David Stewart of the newly founded Celtic Society acted as stylist, dressing the king's distinguished diameter in a Royal Stuart kilt. George Hunter, clothier of 25 Princes Street, no doubt rubbed his hands in glee as he presented a bill for £1,354.18s.0d for 'Highland accoutrements', including the Royal Stuart tartan for the jacket, shoulder plaid and kilt, a baldrick (belt), a pair of Highland pistols, a Highland dirk (short dagger), purse, and powder-horn.

Ceiling of the Crush Hall in the Assembly Rooms, George Street.

Above: Statues in Coade stone now standing in the Crush Hall of the Assembly Rooms.

Right: Interior, Assembly Rooms.

Known for his 'meddling', William Burn added the pompous portico to the original Assembly Rooms (John Henderson, 1787) in 1817 but happily the principal interiors, including the grand salon upstairs, remain more or less intact. It was at a Theatrical Fund Dinner in the Assembly Rooms on 23 February 1827 that Alexander Maconochie, Lord Meadowbank, outed Sir Walter Scott as the author of *Waverley*. It was no surprise to many. More surprising might have been the illicit cock-fighting contests of earlier years held in the kitchens!

No. 45 GEORGE STREET, with its iconic colonnade at ground level, was the former premises of *Blackwood's Edinburgh Magazine*. William

Blackwood (1776–1834) decided to move from 17 Princes Street to George Street in 1829, writing to his son in India that George Street was more commercial and 'the east end of Princes Street, is now like Charring [sic] Cross, a mere place for coaches'. His brother Thomas, a silk merchant, moved next door and in 1830 Thomas Hamilton re-modelled the entire frontage of both premises.

Further along, just before Frederick Street and the **STATUE OF WILLIAM PITT THE YOUNGER** (1833), **60 GEORGE STREET** is marked with a plaque commemorating the visit in 1811 of the radical romantic poet Shelley while on honeymoon with his first wife, Harriet Westbrook.

Alongside established architects, the builder-architect was a key player in the building of the New Town. James Nisbet (d.1811) started out as a plasterer, then became a builder and designed the **TONTINE HOUSE** (1792) at Nos 120–24 George Street. The building was never completed and served as an army barracks during the Napoleonic Wars.

Across the way, **133 GEORGE STREET** was the home of one of the great practical men of the Enlightenment, Sir John Sinclair, who produced the *Statistical Account of Scotland* in 1790, based on accounts provided by 938 parish ministers throughout the country. In 1755 parish ministers

Above: Statue of William Pitt the Younger (1759–1806) by Sir Francis Chantrey (1833).

Below: Tontine House, now offices at 120–124 George Street.

had helped Alexander Webster, Minister of the Tolbooth Church, to prepare a census which showed 48,815 residents in Edinburgh. The first official census in Britain was in 1801.

Sir Walter Scott's house at **39 CASTLE STREET** is an example of the Scottish-European tenement hidden behind a double bow-fronted Georgian house. He lived there for most of his married life and kept his mother close by at **75 GEORGE STREET**, where she died in 1819.

Charlotte Square

One of the finest urban spaces in Europe, **CHARLOTTE SQUARE** is Robert Adam's most influential contribution to the New Town. Given the haphazard style of building up to the late 1780s and the New Town residents' distaste of encroaching commerce on Princes Street and George Street, the town council decided that Charlotte Square should be an architectural showpiece. Initial elevations for a square from Robert Kay and James Nisbet were rejected in 1791 in favour of a unified design from Robert Adam. Each side of the square features a palace-front, with the north side being 329 feet (100 metres) 'of uncommon finesse and grandeur' in Craigleith Stone. Adam's seven-bay centrepiece is copied in many later palace-fronts in the New Town.

The land on which **BUTE HOUSE** (6 Charlotte Square) stands, home of the First Minister of Scotland, was sold in 1792 to Orlando Hart, shoemaker, for £290, then sold to Sir John Sinclair in 1806 for £2,950,

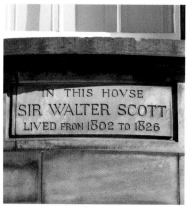

Top: Sir John Sinclair (1754–1835) by John Kay.

Above: Sir Walter Scott's home at 39 Castle St.

> **Elizabeth Grant of Rothiemurchus moves to Charlotte Square**
>
> The diarist Elizabeth Grant of Rothiemurchus, was born at **5 CHARLOTTE SQUARE**, a house built for her parents by the architect-builders Adam and Charles Russell. In later life she moved back there:
>
> In May we removed to Charlotte Square, a house I found the most agreeable of any we had ever lived in in Edinburgh; the shrubbery in front, and the peep from the upper windows behind, of the Firth of Forth with its wooded shores and distant hills, made the look out each way so very cheerful. We were in the midst, too, of our friends. We made two new acquaintances, the Wolfe Murrays next door [No. 17], and Sir James and Lady Henrietta Fergusson [of Kilkerran] in my father's old house in which Jane and I were born [No. 5].

and finally bought by the 4th Marquess of Bute, who gave it to the nation. The central door was necessary for the symmetry of Adam's palace-front, but normally the main door would be on the same side as the main staircase. **THE GEORGIAN HOUSE**, run by the National Trust for Scotland, at No. 7 is open to the public and displays a period interior. Progress on completing Charlotte Square stalled when Adam died in 1792 and so the council commissioned Robert Reid to complete the scheme in 1814.

Having abandoned Robert Adam's elaborate design for a simpler plan by Robert Reid, the foundation stone for **ST GEORGE'S CHURCH**, was laid on 14 May 1811 by the Lord Provost in Charlotte Square. Later that day the party returned to the Old Town to take possession of its new Council Chambers in the Royal Exchange (p. 10). Craig's original New Town plan shows St George's Square at the west end but this was changed in 1786 to Charlotte, in honour of Queen Charlotte.

By the early 19th century the legal profession were well ensconced in Charlotte Square. Robert Adam's nephew, William Adam, Lord Chief Commissioner of the Jury Court, came to No. 31 in 1825, Lord Dundrennan lived at No. 35 while Henry Cockburn had his town house at No. 14 from 1813 to 1848.

Top: The north side of Charlotte Square, which includes Bute House, by Robert Adam.

Above: The west side of Charlotte Square showing St George's Church, now West Register House.

Right: The Theatre Royal, now demolished, was sited at the east end of Princes Street at the North Bridge (from Thomas Shepherd's *Modern Athens*, 1829).

Below: The Scott Monument, the largest monument in the world dedicated to an author.

Opposite left: The Royal Institution, now home to the Royal Scottish Academy.

Opposite right: Sir Walter Scott by Benjamin Crombie.

Princes Street

Merchant John Neale built the first house on Princes Street in 1769 (on a site opposite the Balmoral Hotel) with a clear view of the first pedestrians on the new North Bridge and the oyster lasses yelling 'Caller Ou" outside the **THEATRE ROYAL** on Shakespeare Square. Neither house nor theatre remain. At present commerce rules the city's principal thoroughfare on the north side. Looking southwards to the Old Town skyline remains a welcome diversion.

As the largest monument in the world to a writer, the **SCOTT MONUMENT** honours one of the New Town's most famous residents. Funded by public subscription, with donations from bankers in St Petersburg and William IV, the monument (1844) is 40 feet (12 metres) taller than Nelson's Column in Trafalgar Square and offers dramatic views to anyone willing to climb all 287 steps. It was a carpenter from Peebles, George Meikle Kemp, under the pseudonym of John Morvo, who won the design competition, which included an entry from W.H. Playfair. Close by is Waverley Station, the only railway station in the world named after a book, taking its name from Scott's 1814 work, *Waverley*.

Known as the Royal Scottish Academy (RSA) since 1911, Playfair originally designed the building for the **ROYAL INSTITUTION** in 1822. It was home for many years to the RSE, the Society of Antiquaries and the Royal Institution for the Encouragement of the Fine Arts. A statue

Sir Walter Scott

Imbued with a sense of history and a rational modern outlook, Scott's literary works were a major force in changing the historical philosophy of Europe in the 19th century. His influence was global, touching writers such as Balzac and Pushkin, historians such as Carlyle and Thierry and composers such as Donizetti, Rossini and Bizet.

In the 1820s the highlight of any cultural visit to Scotland was an audience with Sir Walter Scott. Mendelssohn wrote to his mother during his visit in 1829: 'Whether I shall see Sir Walter Scott here, although I have a letter to him from one of his intimate friends in London, is quite uncertain; yet I hope so, chiefly to escape a scolding from you, dear mother, if I return without having seen the lion.'

Like others before him, Scott was a polymath, being a successful lawyer, versifier, novelist, ballad-collector, critic and man of letters. Scott was feted on his many travels, writing to Sir Adam Ferguson from Dublin, 'Here we are in Pat Land . . . and almost killed with kindness . . . The Irish have been most flatteringly kind in their reception.'

During George IV's visit to Edinburgh, Sir Robert Peel noted that Scott's reception in the High Street was the first thing to give him a notion of 'the electric shock of a nation's gratitude'.

William Playfair's National Gallery of Scotland.

'The race of mankind would perish did they cease to aid each other. We cannot exist without mutual help. All therefore that need aid have a right to ask it from their fellow-men; and no one who has the power of granting can refuse it without guilt.'

Sir Walter Scott

'Of all the cities in the British Islands, Edinburgh is the one which presents most advantages for the display of a noble building; and which, on the other hand, sustains most injury in the erection of a commonplace or unworthy one.'

John Ruskin

of Pallas Athena, for whom the Parthenon was built, was proposed by Playfair as the final adornment on the pediment above the grand portico. Queen Victoria, as Britannia, was the final choice, with Egyptian sphinxes by sculptor Sir John Steell set on either side for company.

In the realm of public buildings Playfair reigned supreme and the city's Hellenic vision was realised in large part by him. Stuart and Revett's carefully measured plans and elevations in *The Antiquities of Athens* provided Playfair and Thomas Hamilton, who never visited Greece, with a precise grammar of Greek Classical architecture. Both would have known their friend Hugh 'Grecian' Williams's *Travels in Italy, Greece and the Ionian Islands* (1820) and no doubt they visited his watercolour exhibition of 1822 in Edinburgh.

With his design for **THE NATIONAL GALLERY OF SCOTLAND** (1850–57), Playfair was aware of the scenic demands of the site, the rugged backdrop of the Castle and the requirements of two institutions, the Royal Scottish Academy and the National Gallery. There were entrances at each end of the building, with the RSA in the east wing and the National Gallery in the west wing. The National Gallery took over the entire building in 1911.

The **STATUE OF ALLAN RAMSAY SENIOR** – wigmaker, poet, bookseller, theatre impresario – is an important landmark at the foot of **THE MOUND**, a roadway built on the spoil heap from works in the New Town. His home, now part of Ramsay Garden, is visible behind him, near the Castle.

James Craig's proposal for a canal to replace the drained Nor' Loch was never realised. **EAST PRINCES STREET GARDENS** were developed in the late 1820s with advice from W.H. Playfair and the printer turned naturalist Patrick Neill. The original terrace was widened in the 1840s to accommodate the Scott Monument. In 1820 the artist and architectural antiquarian, James Skene of Rubislaw, a close friend of Sir Walter Scott, planned **WEST PRINCES STREET GARDENS**, no doubt motivated to improve the view from his home at No. 126 Princes Street. The gardens originally ran all the way around the Castle Rock until interrupted by the railway and the building of Johnston Terrace.

A church often makes a pleasing termination for a grand thoroughfare. **ST JOHN'S EPISCOPAL CHURCH** (William Burn, 1818), in Revived Perpendicular style at the west end of Princes Street, was the new home for the congregation of the Charlotte Street Chapel in Rose Street. The revived Gothic interior was new to Scotland, and the Gothic towers and spires were a major contribution to the 19th-century 'Romantic Edinburgh' cityscape. Around the corner in Lothian Road, **ST CUTHBERT'S CHURCH** is mostly 19th century but retains its 18th-century steeple. The graveyards of both these churches merit a stroll, with many

Above: Statue of Allan Ramsay Senior (1713–84) by Sir John Steell, framed by the trees of West Princes Street Gardens.

Below: The home of Allan Ramsay in Ramsay Garden. The building is still visible, slightly right of centre in the modern photograph above.

Above: St John's Episcopal Church, Princes Street, and St Cuthbert's Church, Lothian Road, from Thomas Shepherd's *Modern Athens* (1829).

Opposite left: 1–3 York Place (1824) by David Paton.

18th-century noteworthy graves, including those of Henry Raeburn, Susan Ferrier (St John's), the 14th Earl of Glencairn (friend and patron of Burns) and the artist Alexander Nasmyth (St Cuthbert's).

York Place and Queen Street

In 1824 David Paton, son of John Paton, one of the chief builders of the northern New Town, designed **1–3 YORK PLACE** with notable double-height shop-fronts and continued fenestration on the first floor. He then took his neo-classicism to Raleigh, North Carolina, taking charge of the new State Capitol in 1833 where he installed a Scots-style pencheck stair 'consisting of two elegant stone staircases from the second to the third floors'.

Allan Ramsay Junior committed many early Enlightenment figures such as David Hume and J.J. Rousseau to canvas in the mid-18th century. Later it was Sir Henry Raeburn who indulged the landed, professional and mercantile classes who sat in his red velvet chair at **32 YORK PLACE** (p. 60) for their portrait. Many of Raeburn's portraits can be seen nearby in **THE SCOTTISH NATIONAL PORTRAIT GALLERY.**

'Such was my first view of Edinburgh. I descended again into her streets in a sort of stupor of admiration.'

J.G. Lockhart in *Peter's Letters to his Kinsfolk* (1819)

Son of the Enlightenment: James Nasmyth

James Nasmyth (1808–90) was enlightened and practical. Born and educated in Edinburgh, by the age of 19 he had built a road steam-carriage that could be considered a precursor to the car. He describes it thus: 'The steam-carriage was completed and exhibited before the members of the Society of Arts. Many successful trials were made with it on the Queensferry Road, near Edinburgh. The runs were generally of four or five miles, with a load of eight passengers sitting on benches about three feet from the ground.'

As the Industrial Revolution progressed, James Nasymth's inventions such as the steam hammer and pile driver were key to many new industrial processes. In later life he became interested in astronomy and photography, becoming a close friend of the painter and photographer, David Octavius Hill.

'He was an all-round man. He had something of the Universal about him. He was a painter, an architect, and a mechanic.' It might be hard to guess the identity of this polymath but James Nasmyth's comment on his father Alexander is typical of many Enlightenment figures. Alexander Nasmyth, known first as the father of landscape painting in Scotland, also designed St Bernard's Well in Stockbridge (p. 87) and submitted a design for the Nelson monument (p. 98). He entertained many at his home at **47 YORK PLACE**, soirées described by

Above. Raeburn House, studio of Sir Henry Raeburn, at 32 York Place.

Below. 8 Queen Street by Robert Adam, 1771.

Below right. Statue of Hygeia, Aesculapius and Hippocrates at the entrance of the Royal College of Physicians, Queen St.

his son James as 'unostentatious and inexpensive gatherings of friends' that included a broad spectrum of talents from art to engineering.

Open views all the way down to the Firth of Forth compensated for the cold northerly aspect of Queen Street, the longest 18th-century terrace in the New Town. The grandest house, possibly the first in the street, and certainly the first to have two drawing rooms, was **8 QUEEN STREET** (Robert Adam, 1771), built for Robert Orde, Chief Baron of the Scottish Exchequer. In 1793 Orde's daughter Elizabeth accepted the brusque marriage proposal of an elderly Lord Braxfield, whose very name 'smacked of the gibbet' (Braxfield was infamously known as 'the hanging judge'), while her sister Nancy gained the admiration of David Hume but alas no further engagement. However Hume did bequeath ten guineas to her, 'to buy a ring, as a Memorial of my Friendship and Attachment to so amiable and accomplished a person'.

Next door is **THE ROYAL COLLEGE OF PHYSICIANS** (f.1681), a fine neo-classical design by Thomas Hamilton built in 1844 to replace Physicians' Hall in George Street (pp. 47–48) . Statues of Hygeia, Aesculapius and Hippocrates adorn the grand portico. Nos 8 and 9 were joined together in 1957 and later sympathetically restored with reference to Adam's designs for Baron Orde's house.

No. 28 QUEEN STREET was the home of Robert Allan, a wealthy banker and proprietor of the *Caledonian Mercury*, based in Old Fishmarket Close in the Old Town. Further west at No. 62 lived the

mathematician and physicist, Professor John Leslie. In 1802 Leslie gave the first modern explanation of capillary action and a few years later showed how an air-pump could be used for the artificial production of ice. The only house in the street to rival the elegant residence of Baron Orde was at No. 64, a grand townhouse built in 1790 for the 7th Earl of Wemyss.

New Town lighting

In 1787 one Writer to the Signet, John Hunter of 4 Queen Street, was the first to get permission to install an iron lamp standard at his home in place of the unstable and ugly wooden lamp posts. Until gas lighting arrived around 1817 houses were lit by oil lamps. Fuelled by Greenland whale oil 'and two wicks of sixteen threads of the best Oxford cotton', they were mounted on decorative wrought or cast-iron lamp standards. The link horns used by the link boy to extinguish his torch are still visible at many doorways. By the early 1820s most lamps in the city centre were gas-lit, with the very last gas lamp turned off in Ramsay Garden in 1965.

No. 64 Queen St, built in 1790 for the 7th Earl of Wemyss

'At No. 53 [Queen Street] lived Mrs Wilson, the mother of "Christopher North" [John Wilson], another of those splendid old dames peculiar to Edinburgh, upholders of Church and State to the bitter end, perfect housekeepers, and capable of ruling family and servants with the unquestioned sway of a benevolent autocrat.'

Mary D. Steuart, *The Romance of the Edinburgh Streets* (2nd edition 1929)

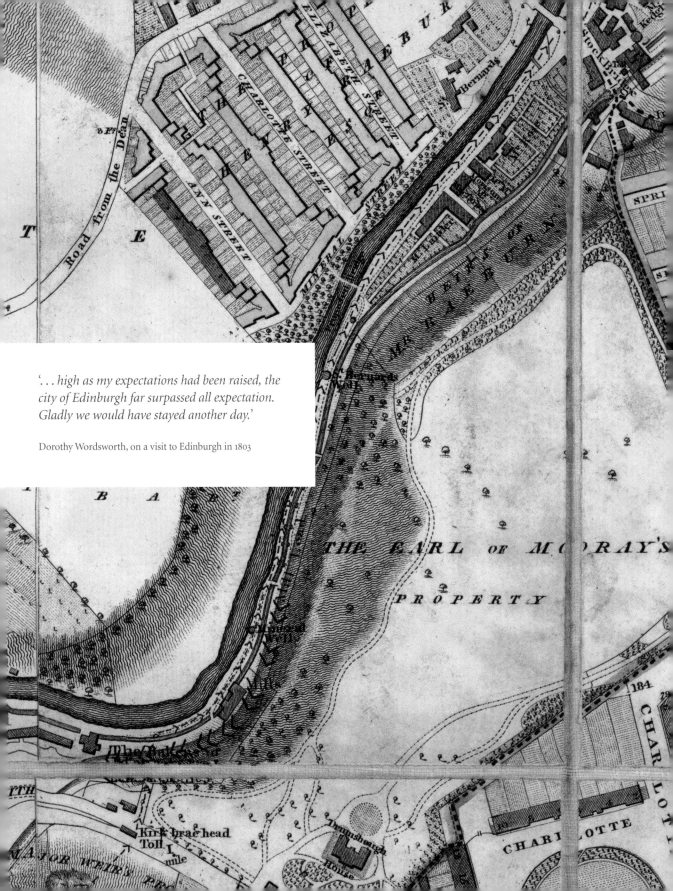

'. . . high as my expectations had been raised, the city of Edinburgh far surpassed all expectation. Gladly we would have stayed another day.'

Dorothy Wordsworth, on a visit to Edinburgh in 1803

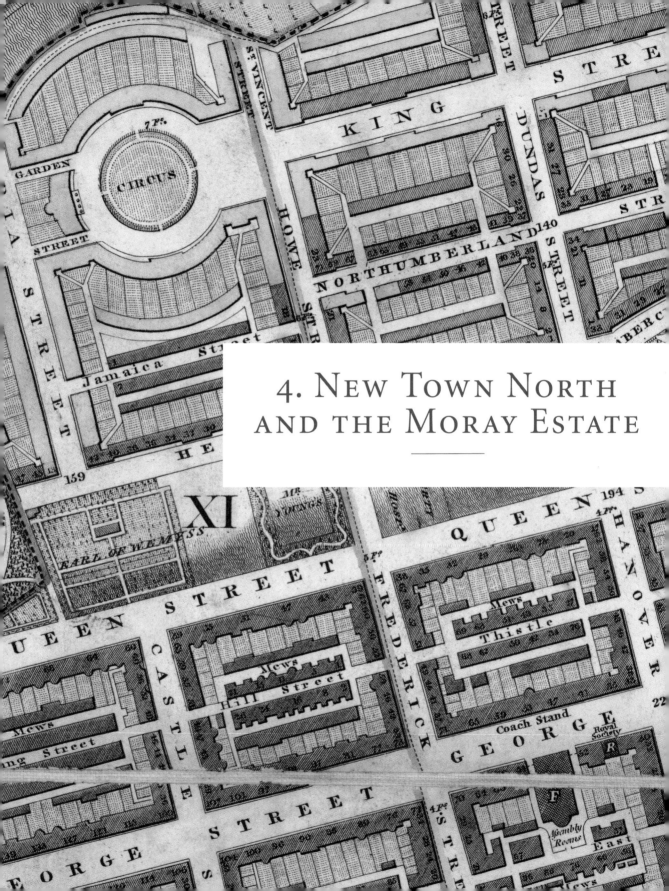

4. New Town North and the Moray Estate

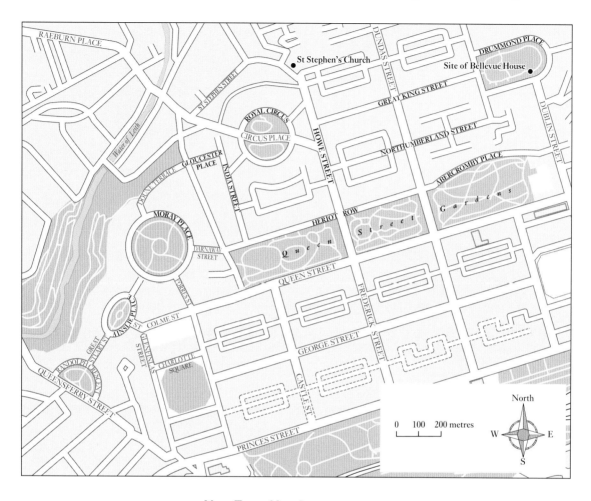

New Town North

By 1801, the New Town was heading northwards and downhill. One of the first to realise the potential of this area was David Steuart (1747–1824), Lord Provost from 1780 to 1782, who moved to 5 Queen Street in 1780 and quickly acquired several acres to the north.

Steuart's financial difficulties in 1800 meant his lands were sold to others who, with the Heriots Hospital Trust and the town council, adopted Robert Reid and William Sibbald's revised plan of 1802 for the northern New Town. The grand central avenue of **GREAT KING STREET** (originally King Street) formed the east–west axis from Bellevue in the east to the boundary of the Moray Estate in the west. Given the success of Adam's designs in Charlotte Square, the council demanded all further developments in the New Town have architect-designed elevations. As

Left: Great King Street.

Below: Plaque at 84 Great King Street to Felix Yaniewicz.

a result the northern New Town was the largest single scheme of the Georgian city and today retains an admirable amount of architectural integrity.

One of the busiest builders in the northern New Town, John Paton, lived at 66 Great King Street, an avenue where the elegance of the palace-block, so successful in Charlotte Square, comes into its own. At 84 Great King Street lived Feliks Yaniewicz, a Polish musician and composer who helped present the city's first music festival in 1815, a forerunner of today's Edinburgh International Festival. Almost 9,000 tickets were sold for this event, with profits going to the Royal Infirmary and the Lunatic Asylum. Yaniewicz lived in Great King Street for over 20 years until his death in 1848. He is buried in Warriston cemetery close to another famous countryman, the Calvinist politician, nationalist and historian Count Valerian Krasinski (1795–1855), who spent his last years in exile in Edinburgh.

With its open sunny prospect, **HERIOT ROW** (p. 66) was quickly feued, proving popular with the legal fraternity, and by 1808 the street was almost complete. The private **QUEEN STREET GARDENS** were not laid out until 1823, too late for Elizabeth Grant of Rothiemurchus, who noted in her memoirs that when her family moved to 8 Heriot Row in 1814 there were no 'prettily laid out gardens opposite: only a long strip

'His tone is pure and equal, his intonation remarkably exact, and his style free from those unmeaning harlequinades, and flattering frippery embellishments, which disfigure the violin playing of so many performers whose merits are otherwise considerable.'

Description of Feliks Yaniewicz's playing in *A Dictionary of Musicians* (1827)

of unsightly grass, a green, fenced by an untidy wall and abandoned to the use of the washer-women'.

As the first shallow crescent to be built in the New Town, the north side of **ABERCROMBY PLACE** attracted attention and some famous residents. W.H. Playfair lived at No. 17 Abercromby Place before moving to 43 Heriot Row. James Pillans, 'one of the fine old Edinburgh Liberals', according to James Nasmyth, lived at No. 22 in the 1830s. After many years as Rector of the old High School, where he invented the blackboard, he took the Chair of Humanity at the University of Edinburgh, a post he held for over 40 years. James Russell, Professor of Clinical Surgery at Edinburgh, lived at No. 30 while a close neighbour at no. 32 was the artist John Syme, a pupil of Raeburn. W.H. Lizars commissioned Syme to paint the famous American wildlife artist J.J. Audubon during his visit to Edinburgh in 1826. The portrait is now part of the White House Art Collection.

DRUMMOND PLACE is named after the visionary Lord Provost

A medical pioneer

While the flow of gentry to the New Town swelled into a flood in the early 19th century, one eminent medic, a resident of **44 HERIOT ROW**, was aware of the plight of less fortunate citizens in Enlightenment Edinburgh. William Pulteney Alison (1790–1859) had witnessed the poverty that still existed in the city as a physician at the New Town Dispensary (1815) and soon recognised the link between poverty and disease. In *Observations on the management of the poor in Scotland and its effect on the health in the Great Towns* (1840), Alison argued that the state must have a major role in the alleviation of poverty rather than religious groups and private charities. As a philosopher, he questioned the parameters of social medicine, but as a physician he implemented practical solutions such as vaccination for smallpox and the Edinburgh Fever Board to combat epidemics. Today Alison is recognised worldwide as one of the great pioneers of epidemiology. Alison's father was the Rev. Archibald Alison (1757–1839), author of *Essays on the Nature and Principles of Taste* (1790).

George Drummond, but he would not recognise the site of his former home today. Drummond Lodge, where he spent his last years, was demolished in the 1770s, as was **BELLEVUE HOUSE**, which once stood on the land now occupied by Drummond Place Gardens. Former residents of Drummond Place include the antiquarian Charles Kirkpatrick Sharpe, who died at No. 28 in 1851, and Adam Black, publisher, who died in 1874 at No. 38. Lots of granite setts (paving) still survive in the roadway here, as do many of the Georgian railings.

To the west is **HOWE STREET**, which retains some good examples of pilastered shops. No. 9 should be remembered as the home of Thomas Hamilton, architect of so many fine buildings in the city, not least the Royal High School. He died here in 1858. W.H. Playfair has made his mark at the bottom of the hill with **ST STEPHEN'S CHURCH** (1827–8), 'a design of vast scale, Baroque power and Grecian severity' neatly blocking out any vista to William Burn's new Edinburgh Academy (pp. 87–88).

Reid and Sibbald had proposed an east–west roadway continuing

Opposite top: Heriot Row.

Opposite bottom: Charles Kirkpatrick Sharpe, antiquarian (1781–1851), resident of Drummond Place, by Benjamin Crombie.

Below: Bellevue House.

from Great King Street downhill to Stockbridge, but W.H. Playfair took another approach and his plan for **ROYAL CIRCUS** prevailed, with the two crescents completed in 1823. One of the first residents, who lived at 21 Royal Circus, was Professor Robert Jameson, Professor of Natural History at Edinburgh for over 50 years and curator of what became in 1812 the Royal Museum of the University. To Jameson, the collection was 'not a private department of the university but a public department connected in some degree with the country of Scotland'. To Charles Darwin, who found student life Edinburgh tedious, the sole effect of Jameson's lectures was the intention, 'never as long as I lived to read a book on Geology or in any way to study the science'. Nearby at **14 INDIA STREET**, is the birthplace of one of the world's greatest scientists, James Clerk Maxwell. During his schooldays and early university years in Edinburgh, James lived with his Aunt Isabella at 31 Heriot Row.

A plaque at **10 GLOUCESTER PLACE** marks the home of John Wilson, a founder of *Blackwood's Edinburgh Magazine* and for 30 years Professor of Moral Philosophy at the University of Edinburgh. Over half of the 71 'Noctes Ambrosianae' pieces published in *Blackwood's Magazine* from 1822 to 1835 were penned by Wilson, with others by James Hogg, J.G. Lockhart and William Maginn. The characters in this 'trenchant satire on men and things in the metropolis of Scotland' were Christopher North (based on Wilson), Timothy Tickler (based on

Opposite (top left): St Stephen's Church.

Opposite (top right): Royal Circus, from Thomas Shepherd's *Modern Athens,* 1829.

Opposite (bottom): John Wilson (1785–1854) founder of *Blackwood's Edinburgh Magazine.*

Left: Mary Somerville (1780–1872), mathematician and scientist after whom Somerville College, Oxford was named.

Below: George Combe (1788–1858), phrenologist.

Wilson's uncle, the lawyer Robert Sym) and the Ettrick Shepherd (based on James Hogg).

Though smaller than the houses in Heriot Row, the properties in **NORTHUMBERLAND STREET** were completed between 1807 and 1819 to a high standard. No. 25 was the home of Sir Walter Scott's biographer, J.G. Lockhart. Lockhart had an interest in phrenology or 'skullology', as Scott called it, and sold No. 25 to Andrew and George Combe who, in 1820, founded the Edinburgh Phrenology Society. George Combe married Cecilia, daughter of the famous actress Sarah Siddons, and his later homes were at 23 Charlotte Square and 45 Melville Street in the West End. The first woman, other than a royal, to appear on a Royal Bank of Scotland banknote was the Scottish mathematician Mary Somerville. Widowed in 1807, she moved to the home of her father, Vice-Admiral Sir William George Fairfax at 53 Northumberland Street. In 1812 she married William Somerville and later moved to London. In 1835, she and Caroline Herschel became the first women members of the Royal Astronomical Society. Somerville College, Oxford is named after her. Professor Robert Christison (1797–1882), a pioneer of modern nephrology, pharmacology and jurisprudence, lived at 63 Northumberland Street. His appearance was 'as distinguished as his reputation' and his influence held great sway against Sophia Jex-Blake and her campaign to admit women into medical school at the University of Edinburgh.

Enlightenment women

Men did not have it all in Enlightenment Edinburgh. Although the Church, law and academia were monopolised by men and insidious chauvinism ruled the Masonic lodges and other clubs and societies, many women did engage in intellectual discussion in Edinburgh drawing rooms.

Alison Rutherford Cockburn (1713–94), poet and songwriter, and later Elizabeth Hamilton (1758–1816), essayist and novelist, were active hostesses in Edinburgh in the 18th century. It was said that Hamilton's house 'was the resort, not only of the intellectual, but of the gay and even of the fashionable and her cheerfulness, good sense and good humour, soon reconciled everyone to the literary lady'. Scott wrote of Alison Cockburn that 'she maintained the rank in the society of Edinburgh which French women of talents usually do in that of Paris'. Hume championed

'unfettered female intellectual enquiry' and Lord Kames included a chapter on 'The Progress of the Female Sex' in his *Sketches of the History of Man*.

Women in polite society were well educated and had access to print in many forms: learned books, novels such as *Pamela* (1741) and *Clarissa* (1747), magazines like the *Ladies Magazine* and periodicals such as the *Edinburgh Review*. Not every Georgian lady was obsessed with the new pattern books and shopping catalogues. For those that chose to publish, for the most part they did so anonymously, as many men had done before them, including Sir Walter Scott. Susan Ferrier's identity as the author of her novels became more widely known, or guessed, during her lifetime, but she always denied it in public: 'I will never avow myself . . . I could not bear the fuss of authorism!'

The Moray Estate

In 1822 the 'multiplication of feuing feet' (Lord Cockburn) were heading to the 13-acre (5.3-ha.) Drumsheugh Estate, 'an open field of as green turf as Scotland could boast of' above the Water of Leith owned by the 10th Earl of Moray. The New Town was moving in a new direction in both shape and form. The Earl of Moray watched the New Town creep up on his estate boundaries and was determined that any development on his land would adhere to strict rules. The 'Articles and Conditions of Roup and Sale of the Grounds of Drumsheugh', dated 7 July 1822, were in many respects a set of early planning regulations. They required feuars to adhere to the architect's plans, to use certain sandstones, to pay for the houses, streets, pavements, boundary walls and pleasure grounds, and hand over to Lord Moray an annual feu duty. Any commercial use was expressly forbidden. The average annual feu duty paid to Lord Moray was about £30, and £2,000 to £3,000 was the average price paid by buyers for a house. To top it all, the builders who took on these feus and conditions had the added inconvenience of carting all the sandstones over the Water of Leith, through the Dean Village and up Bell's Brae. Only in 1832 did Thomas Telford make their lives easier with the building of the Dean Bridge (pp. 76–77).

For his part, Lord Moray commissioned a design from James

'. . . the most extraordinary woman in Europe – a mathematician of the very first rank with all the gentleness of a woman . . . She is also a great natural philosopher and mineralogist.'

Sir David Brewster writing about Mary Somerville in 1829

'*. . . this beautiful plan . . . resulted in the formation of Moray Place, Gloucester Place, Ainslie Place and other parts and pendicles thereof, so well calculated to support the character of Edinburgh as a 'city of palaces'.*

William Scott Douglas commenting in Crombie's *Modern Athenians* on James Gillespie Graham's plan for the Moray Estate

Moray Place.

Gillespie Graham, an established architect who had laid out the Warriston Estate (1807) further east along the Water of Leith. Graham's plan was a masterful feat of urban planning. Had he had aerial views of the terrain, he could not have created a better design to link the Moray feu with the northern and central areas of the New Town. Forgoing the familiar grid and square layout, impractical on this sloping site, he created a series of ovals and crescents that flowed from Randolph Place to Ainslie Place and Moray Place via Great Stuart Street. Radiating from the grandeur of Moray Place, Forres Street, Darnaway Street and Doune Terrace then connected the earlier New Towns.

The resulting showpiece was **MORAY PLACE**, a twelve-sided circus,

James Gillespie Graham (1776–1855)

One of Scotland's most prolific architects, James Gillespie had 'the good luck to secure a tochered lady in marriage', prompting him in 1825, as a gesture to William Graham of Orchill, father of his wife Margaret Anne, to take the name of Graham. His work ranged from grand castellated houses such as Duns Castle (1818) to detailed Gothic churches such as the Tolbooth Church on Castlehill (1839) for which design he had the assistance of A.W. Pugin. In addition to the Moray feu design, he prepared plans for Warriston Crescent and the Blacket Estate.

His 1835 plan to restore Holyrood Abbey as a meeting place for the General Assembly of the Church of Scotland was rejected, as was his design entry for the new Houses of Parliament in London. He died at 15 Castle Street, Edinburgh, on 21 March 1855 and was buried in the south-west section of Greyfriars Kirkyard, known as the Covenanters' Prison, which is accessible on request.

'That the purchasers shall be at the sole expense of forming, causewaying, and paving the streets in front of their respective buildings and meuse lanes opposite to, or in any way connected with, their properties, and shall also make and construct the common sewers, agreeably to a plan to be made out by the same James Gillespie, or other architect to be appointed as aforesaid; and the purchases shall be bound to enclose the areas in Moray Place and Ainslie Place and to lay them down in shrubbery and walls, as shown by the plan.'

Excerpt from 'Articles and Conditions of Roup and Sale of the Grounds of Drumsheugh', 7 July 1822

Below: Ainslie Place.

Opposite bottom: Francis Jeffrey, Lord Jeffrey (1773–1850), critic, judge and resident of Moray Place.

the largest in Edinburgh and one of the longest Georgian terraces in Europe. The grandest house of 11,000 square feet (1,022 square metres) was No. 28, the Earl's own home, while 6,500 square feet (604 square metres) was the norm for adjacent houses. Noteworthy are the six pedimented centrepieces at regular stages around the circus, featuring massive Greek Doric columns and pilastered pavilions. The palace façades are a reference to the Charlotte Square plan (p. 52–53).

AINSLIE PLACE was named after the Earl of Moray's second wife, Margaret Jane Ainslie, daughter of Sir Philip Ainslie of Pilton. Within the Moray feu, other locations were named after family estates, such as Forres Street, Doune Street and Glenfinlas Street. The widow of James Gillespie Graham lived at 1 Ainslie Place after his death. James Gregory (1753–1821), of antacid Gregory's Powder fame, bought No. 10 shortly before his death and his family lived there for many years. William Blackwood, publisher of *Blackwood's Edinburgh Magazine*, kept his distance from his rival at the *Edinburgh Review*, Francis Jeffrey (who lived in Moray Place), with a home at 3 Ainslie Place. Although W.H. Playfair had criticised some of Gillespie Graham's plans for the Moray Feu, it did not stop him moving into 17 Great Stuart Street.

The rigorous terms and conditions of the Moray feu have ensured its survival as an outstanding single plan development in the New Town. A proposal in the 1950s to turn the garden at Randolph Crescent (sold by Lord Moray to its adjacent proprietors in 1865) into a round-about with further destruction of parts of Ainslie Place and Saint Colme Street faced heavy opposition from the feuars. The scheme was abandoned after a public enquiry.

Residents of Moray Place

The strict regulations of the Moray feu would ensure that it became the most desirable address for the bon ton in town. With just 150 homes and no threat of commercial intrusion, the area became popular with the legal elite, retirees from the East India Company and the West Indies, and landed gentry in need of a town residence.

A leisurely stroll around Moray Place in 1829 would have brought you to the town residence of Robert Wardlaw-Ramsay of Tillicoultry at No. 11, next door to John Hope, Solicitor General, at No. 12 and James Hunt of Pittencrieff at No. 13. You might well have seen Francis Jeffrey (right), advocate and editor of the *Edinburgh Review*, stepping down from his new townhouse at No. 24 on his way to No. 47. There he would greet his good friend Sir James Wellwood Moncrieff, Dean of the Faculty of Advocates. A few steps further would find you at the home of Lord Moray, who lived next door to Major General John Cunningham. Dr T.C. Hope, Professor of Chemistry and Chemical Pharmacy at the University of Edinburgh, was close by at No. 31, and at No. 36 lived Sir Patrick Murray of Ochertyre, Baron of Exchequer.

Sir James Wellwood Moncrieff was much in public view in 1829 for speaking out in favour of Catholic Emancipation, becoming a judge of the Court of Session and for taking on the defence of the infamous William Burke at his trial for murder. He died at 47 Moray Place in 1851 and was buried in the Dean Cemetery near his old friend Francis Jeffrey, who had passed away the previous year.

'A city that possesses a boldness and grandeur of situation beyond any that I have ever seen.'

Thomas Pennant,
A Tour in Scotland (1779)

5.
WEST END

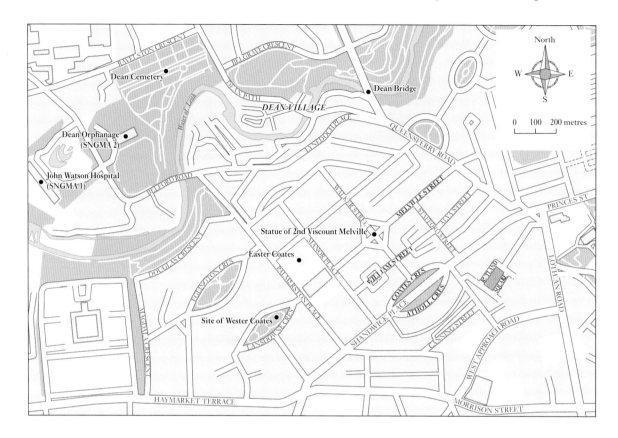

'His gradual rise from the
stonemasons' and builders' yard
to the top of his profession . . . is to
be ascribed not more to his genius,
his consummate ability, and
persevering industry, than to
his plain, honest, straightforward
dealing, and the integrity and
candour which marked his
character throughout life.'

From the obituary of Thomas Telford,
The Scotsman, 6 September 1834

For the builders of the western New Town, it was very much a level
playing field. The terrain presented few design challenges for the architects, but, with several private estates involved, the West End was not
complete until the 1860s.

The most impressive landmark is the **DEAN BRIDGE** (1831–3) by
Thomas Telford (1757–1834). Designs for the Dean Bridge by James
Jardine in 1825 and James Gillespie Graham in 1828 were dismissed by
part-funders the Cramond Road Trustees, who would only pay for a
toll-free bridge designed by Telford.

The major promoter and funder of the Dean Bridge was John
Learmonth of Dean (Lord Provost in 1831), who required access from
the New Town to his Dean Estate. **RUTLAND SQUARE** was built at the
same time as the Dean Bridge for Learmonth by John Tait, with a
revised scheme originally prepared by Archibald Elliot. Tait himself
designed 15 Rutland Square, once the home of Sir Robert Rowand
Anderson (1834–1921), founder and first President of the Royal Institute

of Architects in Scotland (RIAS). Anderson bequeathed the building and its furnishings to the RIAS.

Dean Bridge (1831–3), by Thomas Telford, viewed from the east, just before Dean Village.

The south side of Shandwick Place (formerly Maitland Street) was laid out in 1805. Of much greater interest is **MELVILLE STREET**, the axis of Robert Brown's design for the estate of Sir Patrick Walker. The graceful arched lamp-holders and the serpent lamp extinguishers coiled into

Thomas Telford

Thomas Telford had worked as a stonemason in the New Town in the early 1780s, coincidentally at the same time as his future adversary, the engineer John Rennie, was studying at the University of Edinburgh under Professor John Playfair.

Telford's 'visual thinking' turned daring feats of engineering into awe-inspiring realities all over Britain, from the Caledonian Canal in the Scottish Highlands to the Menai Bridge in Anglesey in Wales. Many of Telford's projects were so big that they required Acts of Parliament to provide the funds. Hailing from the same parish, William Johnstone, later William Pulteney, who had spent many years in Edinburgh, became his great friend and patron. In 1808, he appointed Telford to design the world's largest herring fishing port in Wick, Caithness, known as Pulteney-town.

In his youth, Telford wrote poetry, and Edinburgh publisher Walter Ruddiman published his poem to Robert Burns in his *Weekly Magazine* in 1779:

> *How sweetly flow thy simple strains,*
> *Dear Bard of Scotia's happy plains*
> *Thou pride of a' the cottage swains*
> *None sings like thee.*

His last will and testament recognised a new generation of enlightened talents, with legacies for the engineer James Jardine, the architect W.H. Playfair and the publishers of the *Edinburgh Encyclopaedia*.

Above (clockwise from top left): Rutland Square, William Street, balcony detail of Coates Crescent, Melville Street.

the railings add to the monumental impact of the streetscape here.

Just as in St Andrew Square, 'the Dundas Despotism' made its mark in the West End with a striking **BRONZE OF ROBERT DUNDAS**, 2nd Viscount Melville, by Sir John Steell in Melville Crescent. Robert Saunders-Dundas, only son of Henry Dundas, 1st Viscount Melville, first entered Parliament in 1794 and famously defended his father against impeachment in 1806. In 1812 he became First Lord of the Admiralty, but refused to serve under Prime Minister George Canning in 1827 and resigned. While many considered Robert Dundas authoritarian like his father, Sir Walter Scott wrote to John Murray that,

Sir David Brewster

One of the greatest Enlightenment figures lived at **10 COATES CRESCENT** in the 1820s. David Brewster (1781–1868) was originally destined for the pulpit, but his distaste for public speaking persuaded him in 1801 to pursue his interests in optics and scientific instruments.

As his colleague James Hogg wrote, 'It was a pity for the Kirk . . . but it was a good day for Science . . . for if the doctor had gotten a manse, he might most likely have taken to his toddy like other folk.' Recognised as the leading experimental physicist in Britain, Brewster was also a prolific author, editing the *Edinburgh Encyclopaedia* from 1808 to 1830, the *Edinburgh Philosophical Journal* with Robert Jameson from 1819 to 1824, and providing extensive copy for the *Encyclopaedia Britannica*.

It was Brewster who persuaded his friend, Fox Talbot to patent his new calotype process only in England, so allowing the development of early photography in Scotland. He also introduced the Edinburgh painter David Octavius Hill to one of Fox Talbot's disciples, Robert Adamson.

Brewster is famous for inventing the kaleidoscope but patent piracy (some 200,000 copies were made in one three-month period) prevented him making his fortune from it. Dr Peter Roget, (of *Thesaurus* fame) did compliment his invention in *Blackwood's Edinburgh Magazine* in 1818, stating, 'In the memory of man, no invention, and no work, whether addressed to the imagination or to the understanding, ever produced such an effect.'

Brewster's first wife was Juliet Macpherson (c.1776–1850), daughter of the poet James 'Ossian' Macpherson, and he courted her over supper at the home of Miss Playfair, sister of his great friend and colleague Professor John Playfair.

'Though no literary man he is judicious, clairvoyant, and uncommonly sound-headed, like his father, Lord Melville'.

Parallel to Melville Street is **WILLIAM STREET** (Robert Brown, 1824–5), with Georgian shop fronts complete with cast-iron balconies underneath to entice enthusiastic Georgian window shoppers. The design of **COATES CRESCENT** (Robert Brown, 1813) echoes Abercromby Place, being a divided crescent with flat-fronted pavilions and elegant triple balconies at first-floor level. **ATHOLL CRESCENT**, on the other side, was built later to designs by Thomas Bonnar (1825).

The oldest building in the New Town is probably **EASTER COATES**, a 17th-century laird's house to the north of St Mary's Episcopal Cathedral. Alterations in the 19th century made use of feature stones and windows from demolitions in the Old Town. The house was later part of the legacy of two grand-daughters of Lord Provost George Drummond, Barbara and Mary Walker, to the Scottish Episcopal Church. This legacy enabled St Marys' Cathedral to be built on Palmerston Place.

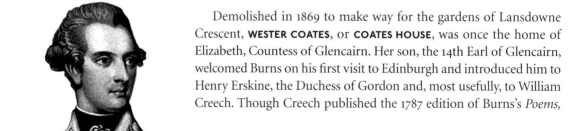

Demolished in 1869 to make way for the gardens of Lansdowne Crescent, **WESTER COATES**, or **COATES HOUSE**, was once the home of Elizabeth, Countess of Glencairn. Her son, the 14th Earl of Glencairn, welcomed Burns on his first visit to Edinburgh and introduced him to Henry Erskine, the Duchess of Gordon and, most usefully, to William Creech. Though Creech published the 1787 edition of Burns's *Poems,*

Chiefly in the Scottish Dialect, Burns was reliant on subscriptions and it was the Earl and Lady Glencairn who encouraged others, including members of the Caledonian Hunt, to subscribe. The 14th Earl died in 1791 in Edinburgh and is buried in St Cuthbert's Graveyard off Lothian Road (p. 58). Burns, conscious of the earl's patronage to him in Edinburgh, presented Lady Cunningham with his 'Lament for James, Earl of Glencairn', declaring to her in a letter of 1791 'my dearest existence I owe to the noble house of Glencairn'.

At the western extremity of the West End and close to the Water of Leith in Belford Road stand two 19th-century buildings forming the Scottish National Gallery of Modern Art. On the west side is an imposing neo-classical building designed by William Burn (1825), built with a legacy from Edinburgh lawyer John Watson, who died in 1762. The **JOHN WATSON HOSPITAL**, for fatherless children of the professional classes, later the John Watson School, was based here from 1828 until its closure in 1975. Across the road is the old **DEAN ORPHANAGE**, known today as Modern Two, originally designed by Thomas Hamilton (1833) as a replacement for the old Orphan Hospital under the North Bridge. The clock above the entrance comes from the Netherbow Port on the Royal Mile, demolished by an 'improving' town council in 1768. It was part of the Orphan Hospital until its demolition in the 1840s.

A walk around the nearby **DEAN CEMETERY**, built on the site of old Dean House, allows the visitor to pay homage to many sons of Enlightenment Edinburgh, including W.H. Playfair, Francis Jeffrey, Henry Cockburn, the architect Thomas Bonnar and David Octavius Hill.

Opposite top: John Watson Hospital, now part of the Scottish National Gallery of Modern Art.

Opposite middle: Dean Orphanage, also now part of the Scottish National Gallery of Modern Art.

Opposite bottom: The 14th Earl of Glencairn.

Left: The grave of Henry Cockburn, Lord Cockburn (1779–1854) in Dean Cemetery.

Above: Grave of George Combe, lawyer and phrenologist. It is said he subjected Miss Siddons to a phrenological examination before their wedding to ensure a suitable marital pairing.

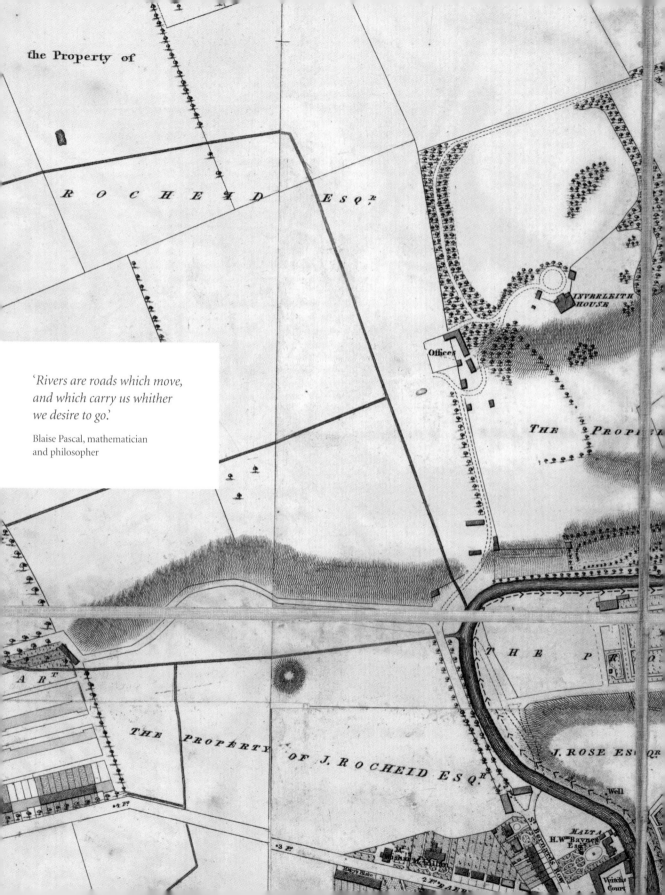

the Property of

R O C H E I D   E S Q.ᴿ

'Rivers are roads which move,
and which carry us whither
we desire to go.'

Blaise Pascal, mathematician
and philosopher

INVERLEITH
HOUSE

Offices

THE   PROPE

THE   P

THE   PROPERTY   OF   J. ROCHEID   ESQ.ᴿ

J. ROSE   ESQ.ᴿ

A R T

Well

MALT A
H. Wᵐ BAYNE
ESQ.

St B
Veitch's
Court

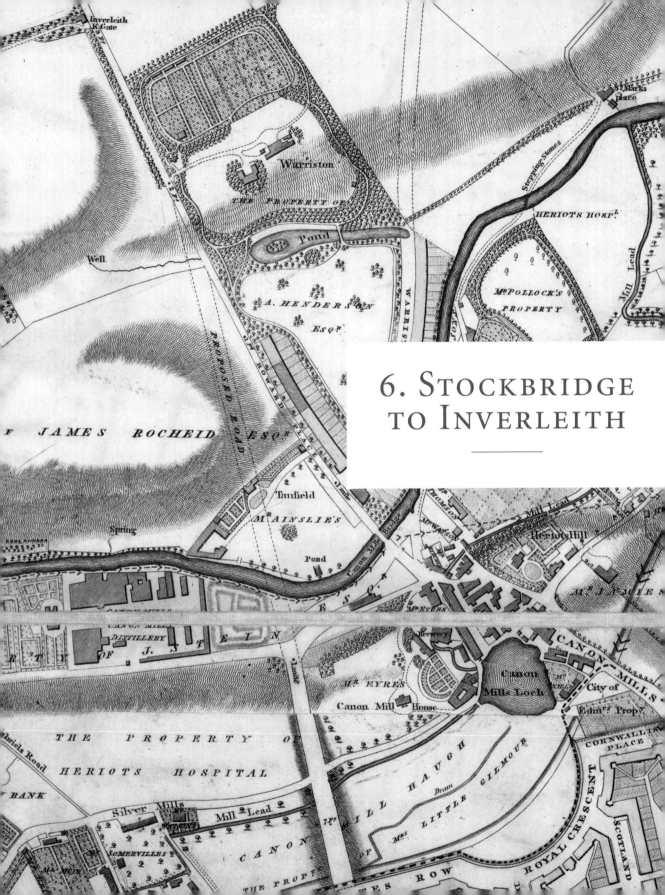

6. STOCKBRIDGE TO INVERLEITH

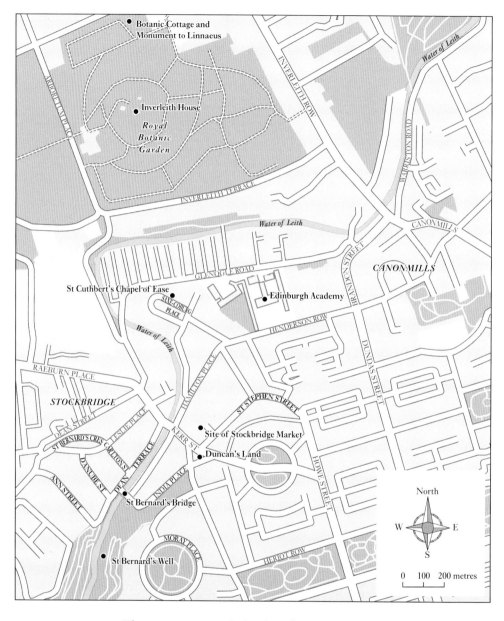

The **WATER OF LEITH**, its banks softened by trees, along with the intimate layout of the streets, allowed Stockbridge to retain its village ambience after development. The original timber or 'stocc brycg' gave the area its name and was replaced in 1801 to allow wheeled traffic to cross the river between the St Bernard's and Deanhaugh estates. These estates were the property of the artist Sir Henry Raeburn, who lived in **ST BERNARD'S**

HOUSE, which originally stood on a site east of **DEAN TERRACE**.

Named after Raeburn's wife, the most elegant street in the Raeburn estate was **ANN STREET** (1814), notable for its elevated site and front gardens, a feature repeated later by its architect, James Milne, in Lynedoch Place in the West End. Milne was chief architect of much of the Raeburn estate and in 1812 published *The Elements of Architecture*, a work owned by Thomas Telford. *The Scots Magazine* noted the publication in 1821 of a new 'Theory of the Earth' by James Milne, architect,

The building blocks of the New Town

Just west of Stockbridge at the Craigleith Retail Park is the **SITE OF CRAIGLEITH QUARRY**, which supplied much of the building stone for the New Town. Operational for more than 300 years, the quarry provided stone for Edinburgh Castle in the 17th century and for Holyrood Palace. Craigleith stone features in many of the city's public buildings, including Old College and Register House, along with some in Charlotte Square and also the National Monument on Calton Hill. When the health hazards for workers amongst the silica-rich sandstone were highlighted, it was suggested that the quarriers grew beards and moustaches to act as filters!

Above left: The Water of Leith, Stockbridge from Thomas Shepherd's *Modern Athens* (1829).

Left: Georgian houses in Ann Street.

The Water of Leith

Rising in the Pentland Hills, the Water of Leith flows 22 miles (35 km) through Edinburgh to the port of Leith. At one time its power was harnessed to drive waterwheels in some 70 mills along the river, producing paper, flour, spices and snuff, as well as woollen and linen cloths. The Water of Leith Walkway is a 12-mile path through the heart of the city, passing close to the Scottish National Gallery of Modern Art, Dean Village, Stockbridge, the Royal Botanic Garden and Leith. The route is suitable for cycling and is partly accessible by wheelchairs and on horseback.

Sir Henry Raeburn (1756–1823)

This great portrait painter of the Enlightenment and the first major Scottish artist to be based at home in Scotland was born in Stockbridge in 1756 and educated at Heriot's Hospital. Encouraged by David Martin and Sir Joshua Reynolds, Raeburn spent time in Italy before returning home in 1787 to set up his studio at 18 George Street. His timing was perfect, as members of the new Edinburgh meritocracy wanted portraits to reflect their status in polite society, and many were willing to pay Raeburn 55 guineas to sit in the red velvet chair in his studio at 32 York Place (p. 60). As the city's physical appearance and social fabric improved, so sitters wanted their portraits to reflect their industriousness, self-reliance and moral fibre. Raeburn later moved to York Place and in 1822 was knighted by George IV during his visit to Edinburgh. He died at St Bernard's House the following year and was buried in St John's Episcopal graveyard, the only graveyard in Edinburgh maintained by an Episcopal church.

Danube Street, Stockbridge.

Edinburgh, but this work appears to be lost in the sands of time.

DANUBE STREET offers two contrasting but very pleasing vistas, rural towards the Water of Leith to the south, while to the north is the grand view to the massive Doric colonnades of **ST BERNARD'S CRESCENT**.

The picturesque **ST BERNARD'S BRIDGE** (1824) leads to **ST BERNARD'S WELL** on the south bank of the Water of Leith, funded by Lord Gardenstone. An eccentric judge who rode a 'jaded steed' to court and had 'the habits of a loose liver', he was highly regarded for his philanthropy. The design by Alexander Nasmyth originally featured a statue of Hygeia made of Coade stone from Georgian entrepreneur Mrs Eleanor Coade's Artificial Stone Manufactory in London. This was replaced with another, carved in 1888 by D.W. Stevenson. Nearby on Gloucester Street the quaint 18th-century **DUNCAN'S LAND** was the birthplace of painter David Roberts (1796–1864), who progressed from theatrical scene painter to make his fortune with topographical views of the Middle East.

One of the most interesting streets in Stockbridge is **ST STEPHEN STREET** (originally Brunswick Street) designed by Robert Brown in the 1820s and featuring pilastered shop fronts similar to his work in William Street in the West End. The higher ground on the south side allowed Brown to create shops on two levels (Nos 22–102), with steps up to one level and steps down to another.

On the north side, the Greek Doric entrances are all that remain of the old **STOCKBRIDGE MARKET** (Archibald Scott, 1824–5), which allowed residents to shop in their local area.

James Milne's scheme for **SAXE-COBURG PLACE** (1821) was not fully completed but **ST CUTHBERT'S CHAPEL OF EASE** (now St Bernard's) was built in 1823 in Saxe-Coburg Street. At this time work was starting close by on the new **EDINBURGH ACADEMY** in Henderson Row by William

Top: St Bernard's Crescent.

Above (left and right): St Bernard's Well, by the Water of Leith just west of Stockbridge.

Top: The Edinburgh Academy in the early 19th century.

Above: The entrance to the old Stockbridge Market, St Stephen Place.

Opposite top left: Botanic Cottage, Royal Botanic Garden.

Opposite top right: Professor John Hope (left) and his gardener, John Williamson, by John Kay.

Opposite bottom: The Monument to Linnaeus (1779), Royal Botanic Garden.

Burn. 'Always Excel' was the motto of the new school, proposed by Henry Cockburn, Leonard Horner, John Russell and Sir Walter Scott, who represented a New Town middle class keen to have their children educated away from the overcrowded Royal High School in the Old Town. A few years later the publicly funded Royal High School would open on Regent Road as a reaction to new fee-paying schools, offering princes and paupers free education in one of the city's finest buildings. The academy's most famous son was James Clerk Maxwell, known as the father of modern physics.

Not far from the Academy, on the north side of the **ROYAL BOTANIC GARDEN (RBGE)** stands one of the earliest Enlightenment classrooms, the **BOTANIC COTTAGE.** Designed by John Adam and James Craig in miniature Palladian style, the cottage originally stood in Leith Walk near the old Botanical Garden. In this building John Hope (1725–86), Professor of Medicine and Botany, taught his students in an upstairs classroom using plant specimens and illustrated diagrams of experiments and plant anatomy. What Hume was to philosophy and Smith to economics, Monboddo to linguistics and Kames to anthropology, Hope was to botany. He was the first to establish the Royal Botanic Garden on a single five-acre (two-ha.) site off Leith Walk in 1763, the first to introduce into Scotland the Linnaean system for cataloguing plants and the first to secure permanent funding for a Regius Keeper

of the Gardens. Hope introduced rhubarb seeds into Scotland and is remembered by the tropical tree genus *Hopea*, named in his honour by his former student, William Roxburgh. The Royal Botanic Garden moved to Inverleith in the early 1820s, with **INVERLEITH HOUSE** (David Henderson, 1774) becoming the residence of the Regius Keeper.

The **MONUMENT TO LINNAEUS** in the Botanic Garden was designed by Robert Adam in 1779 and paid for by Hope himself. The only known likeness of John Hope was captured by John Kay (1742–1826) and includes John Williamson, his chief gardener, who lived in the Botanic Cottage.

At **CANONMILLS** near the Royal Botanic Garden lived Dr Patrick Neill, the distinguished naturalist and first secretary of the Wernerian Natural History Society and the Caledonian Horticultural Society. Neill was head of the city's largest printing firm, Neill & Co., but devoted most of his time to botany and horticulture. He contributed the article on gardening to the 7th edition of the *Encyclopaedia Britannica* and created the scheme for West Princes Street Gardens. Other great Scottish botanists and horticulturalists of the 18th century include John Abercrombie, author of *Every Man His Own Gardener* (1767); Charles Alston, predecessor of John Hope as Superintendent of the Botanic Garden and Professor of Botany and Materia Medica; and Sir James Nasmyth, 2nd Baronet of Dawyck and Posso.

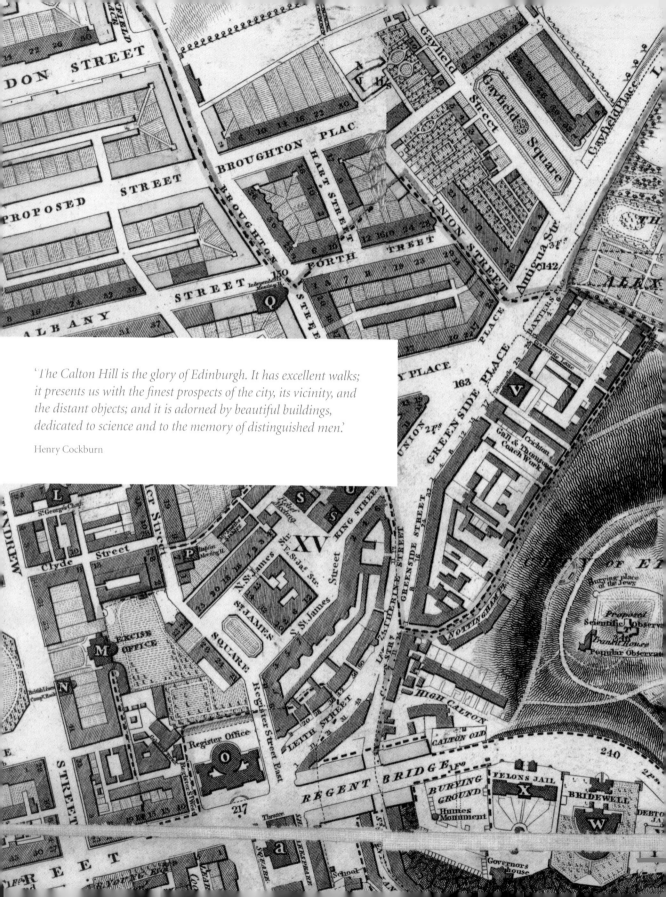

'The Calton Hill is the glory of Edinburgh. It has excellent walks;
it presents us with the finest prospects of the city, its vicinity, and
the distant objects; and it is adorned by beautiful buildings,
dedicated to science and to the memory of distinguished men.'

Henry Cockburn

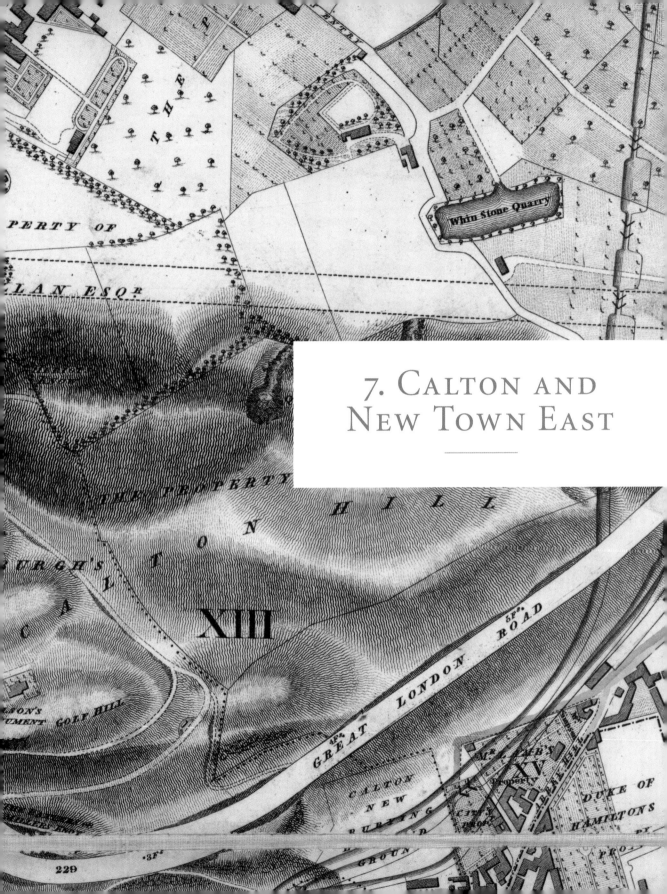

7. Calton and
New Town East

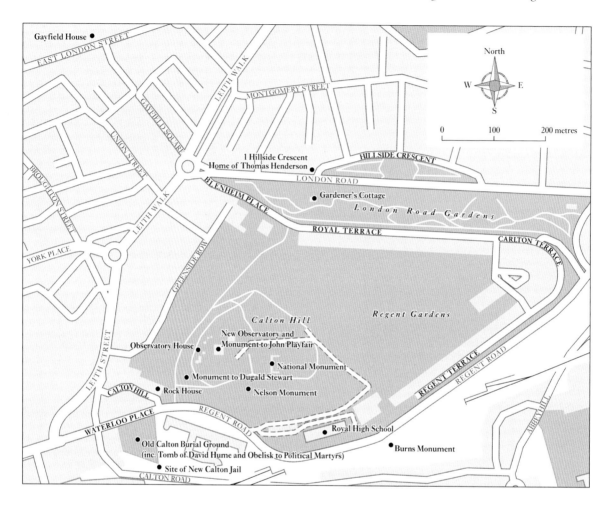

The Act for the building of Calton Road and the Regent Bridge was passed in 1814, primarily to create a route to the New Calton Jail (Archibald Elliott, 1817) being built next door to Robert Adam's Bridewell of 1796. In 1817 the first prisoners were taken from the Tolbooth in the Old Town to the Calton Jail. The Bridewell and Calton Jail were demolished in the 1930s for the building of St Andrew's House. Only the Governor's House (1815) remains; the door to the Death Cell can now be seen in the Beehive Inn in the Grassmarket.

Archibald Elliot's design for **WATERLOO PLACE** (p. 94) consisted of a simple Corinthian triumphal arch with symmetrical buildings in classical style on each side. The open screens offering views to the north and south were an addition by the engineer to the scheme, Robert Stevenson (1772–1850). Stevenson's grand engineering achievement did

Governor's House, originally part of the Calton Jail, which was demolished to make way for St Andrew's House.

not merit a grand fee, however, with his total remuneration less than £900, while Elliott received almost £1,900 for his plans. Arriving in his travelling chariot and barouche with an escort of the 10th Hussars, Prince Leopold of Saxe-Coburg was present for the opening of the Regent Bridge and Waterloo Place in August 1819. Alighting from his carriage at the newly opened Waterloo Hotel (Apex Waterloo Hotel today), he was received by Sir John Marjoribanks, Lord Provost of the city.

The new road cut through the **OLD CALTON BURIAL GROUND**, in the south section of which is the fine neo-classical **TOMB OF DAVID HUME** (p. 94) (Robert Adam, 1777), designed by Scotland's greatest architect for Scotland's greatest philosopher. Hume had commissioned his own monument before his death, a decision described by Adam Smith as 'the greatest piece of vanity I ever saw in my friend Hume'. In stark

'This city is considered as the modern Athens, in politeness, science and literature.'

John Knox, *View of the British Empire*, 1785

'I have devoted myself to the cause of The People. It is a good cause – it shall ultimately prevail – it shall finally triumph.'

Thomas Muir in the Court of Judiciary on 30 August 1793

contrast nearby is the **OBELISK TO THE POLITICAL MARTYRS OF THE 1790s**, who suffered rough justice at the sedition trials of 1793–4 in Edinburgh and Perth.

Sitting aloft from both the Old Town and the New Town, the topography and architecture of **CALTON HILL** provides a dramatic finale to the view eastwards from Princes Street. David Hume appreciated the views from the hill and made a successful petition to the town council in 1775 for the first pleasure walk around the hill, 'for the health and amusement of the inhabitants'. Purchased by the town council in 1724, Calton Hill hosted a variety of activities, ranging from theatre to preaching to public laundry. Access to the hill in the 18th century was

Above: Waterloo Place, south side, from Thomas Shepherd's *Modern Athens* (1829).

Right: David Hume's mausoleum in the Old Calton Burial Ground.

Opposite: Political martyrs of the 1790s remembered at the Political Martyrs Monument, Old Calton Burial Ground. *Left:* Thomas Muir of Huntershill; *right* (top to bottom): Maurice Margarot, William Skirving, Joseph Gerrald, Thomas Fysche Palmer, all by John Kay.

Top: Rock House, the photographic studio of Robert Adamson and David Octavius Hill.

Above: Memorial plaque to James Craig on Observatory House, Calton Hill.

Opposite (top): Above: Observatory House by James Craig (1776).

Opposite (bottom): New Observatory by W.H. Playfair (1818).

via Calton Hill Street, once the home of Burns's great love Clarinda, Mrs M'Lehose, who spent her last years at **No. 14 CALTON HILL**. **ROCK HOUSE** (1750), at the southern end, was the studio of Robert Adamson and David Octavius Hill, pioneers of calotype photography. Hill's second wife, the artist Amelia Paton, was one of the sculptors who created the statues for the Scott Monument on Princes Street.

OBSERVATORY HOUSE (James Craig, 1776) is the oldest of the buildings on Calton Hill and was not completed until 1792. It never functioned as a proper observatory but remains one of Craig's few surviving works. It is now in the care of the Landmark Trust. Thomas Short, optician and brother of the famous telescope-maker James Short, lived there for a time.

Astronomy in Edinburgh flourished with the **NEW OBSERVATORY** by W.H. Playfair in 1818 which became the Royal Observatory during the visit of George IV in 1822. Playfair also dedicated a monument to his uncle John Playfair, Professor of Mathematics at Edinburgh, now incorporated into the wall around the New Observatory. The first Astronomer Royal for Scotland, Regius Professor Thomas Henderson,

Right: National Monument, Calton Hill.

Below: Nelson Monument showing flags flown on Trafalgar Day.

Opposite top: Alexander Nasmyth's design for the Nelson Monument.

Opposite bottom: Monument to Dugald Stewart on Calton Hill, with the Old Town in the background.

was appointed in 1834. The Royal Observatory moved south to Blackford Hill in 1896.

The idea for the **NATIONAL MONUMENT** (1822) was first mooted in 1816 and C.R. Cockerell, who had visited the Acropolis in Athens, was appointed architect, with Playfair as his assistant. It was a grand scheme, designed to commemorate Scottish soldiers and sailors who had died during the Napoleonic Wars, with a budget of £42,000 to be raised by subscription. After 16 months and generous donations from George IV, the Duke of Atholl and Sir Walter Scott, only £16,000 had been raised. The twelve pillars were raised between 1826 and 1829 at a cost of £13,500, leading to 'a striking proof of the pride and poverty of the Scots'. However, Playfair deserves praise for the execution of the twelve beautifully cut pillars of Craigleith stone and 14-foot-high lintels. It is a technical and artistic triumph, and ironically more or less resembles the Parthenon as it is today.

Budget decided the choice of design for the **NELSON MONUMENT** (1807), with Robert Burn's submission winning favour over that of Alexander Nasmyth. In 1815, Thomas Bonnar added the residential section at the base. Above the doorway is Nelson's crest and a model of the HMS *San Josef*, present at the Battle of Cape St Vincent in 1797. A keen eye might spot some movement at the top of the monument on weekdays when the time-signal ball is wound up and duly falls as the One O' Clock Gun is fired at the Castle. The time-signal ball was the idea of Charles Piazzi Smyth, second Astronomer Royal for Scotland, in 1852 and it meant that ship captains in the Forth no longer had to send someone up to town to set their chronometers. On 21 October, the anniversary of the Battle of Trafalgar, Nelson's naval signal, 'England expects this day that every man will do his duty', is flown from the monument.

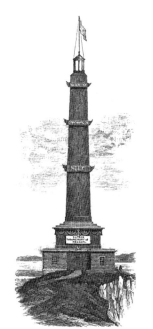

After climbing the 143 steps to the viewing platform, or 'bartizan', on the Nelson Monument, the artist J.M.W. Turner had a superb view of the laying of the foundation stone of the National Monument in 1822 during George IV's visit. The scenes inspired his watercolour 'Edinburgh Castle, March of the Highlanders', now in the Tate Gallery, London.

Playfair's **MONUMENT TO DUGALD STEWART**, the great Professor of Moral Philosophy, commands attention from its vantage point on the hill. Henry Cockburn called his teacher Dugald Stewart 'one of the greatest of didactic orators'.

Without doubt the finest monument of the Greek revival in

Above: The Royal High School (1825–29), the finest monument of the Greek Revival in Scotland.

Opposite top: Burns Monument (1831), detail.

Opposite bottom: Royal Terrace.

'The new High School, one of the most classical and perfect edifices to be seen in Europe, was opened yesterday, under the most favourable auspices.'

The Scotsman 24 June 1829

Scotland and 'one of the finest efforts of architectural art to be found in any city' is Thomas Hamilton's **ROYAL HIGH SCHOOL**. The original idea was for a 'Seminary separate from and altogether independent of the High School of the City' and the first sites to be considered were at Canonmills and in St Andrew Square behind Register House. In the end the school was built on the south face of Calton Hill as part of Edinburgh's Acropolis, at a cost to the town council of £34,000. The Lord Provost hoped that 'instead of deforming this much-admired hill, the building proposed to be erected will form one of the finest pictures in the scene'. It certainly added grandeur to the new eastern approach to the city, possibly surpassing the entry from the south, with Old College, Surgeons' Hall and General Register House.

Pupils at the school were reminded by the headmaster, Dr Aglionby Ross Carson (1780–1850), at the school's opening, that they followed in the footsteps of the illustrious minds of the Enlightenment: 'You are Scotsmen ... yours is the country that gave birth to a Robertson, a Blair, a Hume, a Ferguson, a Reid, a Smith, a Stewart, and when these, and other admired geniuses of former days, are recalled to your memory, let their honoured names fire your ambition and animate you to the most strenuous exertions in a similar career of glory.'

On the south side of Regent Road, a very un-Grecian poet such as

Burns would perhaps be amused at the very Grecian **BURNS MONUMENT** (1831), a tribute promoted by a learned committee that included Sir Walter Scott, Henry Cockburn and Lord Jeffrey. The monument was inspired by the Choragic Monument of Lysicrates in Athens, first depicted in Stuart and Revett's *The Antiquities of Athens* and traditionally associated with poetry and music. The marble statue by John Flaxman (finished by Thomas Denman) that was once inside the Burns Monument is now in the Scottish National Portrait Gallery.

Viewed from the air and looking westwards, **ROYAL TERRACE**, **REGENT TERRACE** and **CARLTON TERRACE**, hang like an elegant necklace around Calton Hill. W.H. Playfair's scheme of 1819, for the eastern extension of the New Town, took account of William Stark's comments that any plan should consider the natural contours of the hill, include trees and exploit the splendid open views.

With their open aspect to Arthur's Seat, houses in Regent Terrace

Dr Patrick Neill (1776–1851), printer and botanist. Secretary of the Caledonian Horticultural Society, 1809–1850.

Residents of Regent Terrace

Notable residents in Regent Terrace in the early 19th century included the prolific Edinburgh engraver W.H. Lizars, who lived at No. 3 and whose work is evident in numerous editions of Scott's works. In his later years the Rev. George Baird, Principal of the University, moved to Regent Terrace to live with his daughter. Though not an intellectual colossus like William Robertson, during his tenure as Principal, from 1793 to 1840, student numbers increased from 1,000 to 2,000 and new Chairs were created in conveyancing, music, forensic medicine, clinical surgery, military surgery and pathology.

The instrument maker Alexander Adie lived at No. 10 but later moved to Carlton Terrace, both houses a short walk from his premises in Princes Street. Born in Edinburgh in 1774, Adie was a famous maker of barometers and scientific instruments, including the sympiesometer, which he patented in 1818. He and his son John were the first scientific instrument makers to be elected to the Royal Society of Edinburgh.

feued quickly in the 1820s, while Royal Terrace was not fully complete until 1860. Playfair's plan extended downhill to **BLENHEIM PLACE**, but construction stopped halfway along Hillside Crescent in 1838 on account of geological problems and a dispute over poor-rates to be paid by feuars. **REGENT GARDENS**, the largest of the New Town gardens still in private ownership, were laid out in the 1830s by Professor Robert

Left: Gayfield House (c.1765).

Below: William Butter, 18th-century property developer (left), in conversation with Sir John Morrison, by John Kay.

Graham and Dr Patrick Neill. Pleasure grounds in the New Town were created primarily for the benefit of local residents. Their creation took considerable time and negotiation on account of the many stakeholders involved, some even set up with an Act of Parliament. Despite most of the gardens being open only to keyholders, they are an important feature of the New Town.

Beyond the grand palace fronts of Royal Terrace are **LONDON ROAD GARDENS**, with the **GARDENER'S COTTAGE** designed by Playfair in 1836. Across the road at **1 HILLSIDE CRESCENT** is the former home of Thomas Henderson (1798–1844), Scotland's first Astronomer Royal; Henderson, one of Britain's most famous astronomers, was the first person to measure parallax and to determine the distance to the stars.

Further on is **GAYFIELD HOUSE**, built c. 1765 by William Butter on a five-acre site overlooking fields and orchards, with views to the hills of Fife. Butter sold the property at a handsome profit to Lord Erskine, son of the Jacobite Earl of Mar, and it later passed to David Leslie, 6th Earl of Leven.

'*The progress of the arts and science is greatly
accelerated by the history of antiquity and of nature.*'

Rev. David Ure (1750–98),
'father of Scottish paleontology'

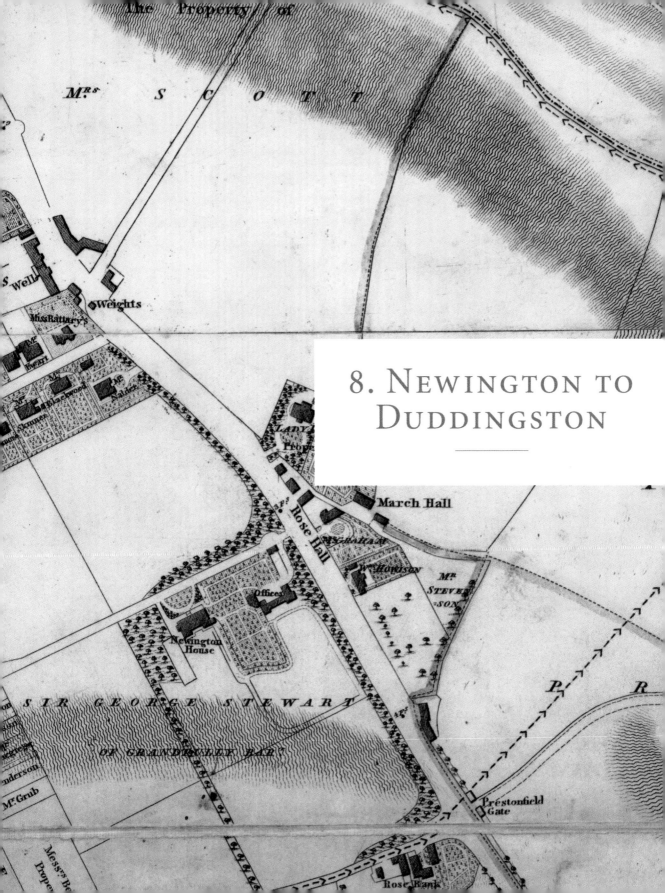

8. NEWINGTON TO DUDDINGSTON

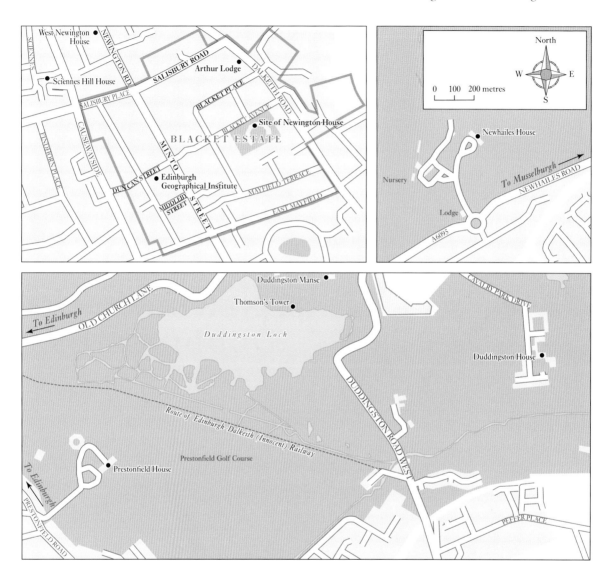

While the New Town advanced northwards, the South Bridge (1788)
provided a direct link between the Old and New Towns and the lands
beyond Nicolson Street to the south. For citizens aspiring to tree-lined
avenues and grand detached villas with gardens in the early 19th
century, the road led south to Newington, and the Blacket Estate.
Purchased in 1803 by eminent surgeon and shrewd speculator Benjamin
Bell, the Blacket Estate was the first development in Edinburgh to give
true country-style living within easy reach of the city centre. With more
than 90 listed buildings of historic or architectural importance, the

Blacket Conservation Area remains a fine early suburb of detached and semi-detached Georgian and Victorian villas.

Enlightenment luminaries had been entertained on the south side for many years by Adam Ferguson at his famous Sunday gatherings at **SCIENNES HILL HOUSE**. Sir Walter Scott described the gathering as 'the most distinguished literati of the old time who still remained, with such young persons as were thought worthy to approach their circle, and listen to their conversation'. A young Walter Scott met Robert Burns there in 1786, a scene he recalled in later years, when Burns rewarded him 'with a look and a word, which, though in mere civility, I then received, and still recollect, with great pleasure'. The other guests in the room that day were Adam Smith, Joseph Black, James Hogg, James Hutton, Dugald Stewart, John Home and Scott's lifelong friend Adam Ferguson junior, later Sir Adam Ferguson (p. 108). For those visiting in 1778, there would have been much to discuss at Sciennes Hill House after Adam Ferguson's trip to America as secretary of the Peace Commission.

WEST NEWINGTON HOUSE (c.1805) at 10 Newington Road stands out with its Roman Doric door piece and tripartite windows in which new panes were inserted in 1829. It also has a notable example of a pencheck (Old Scots 'piend check') staircase with ironwork balustrades, a notable feature of New Town houses (p. 108). Each step is a separate piece of stone which interlocks with the treads above and below. By comparison a true cantilevered staircase has each tread fixed at one end with no supports between the treads.

The south side home of William Blackwood (1776–1834) was at **2 SALISBURY ROAD** (1815, with later alterations). He was publisher of

In 1825, new feus in the Blacket Estate were advertised in the *Edinburgh Evening Courant*:

'These lands command the best access and drainage and are supplied with water from public pipes . . . [they are] within the bounds of police, and are well watched and lighted. For the benefit of the feuars it has been resolved to keep present approaches and porters' lodges in Minto Street and Dalkeith Road which will secure to the several lots within the gates all the privacy and convenience of country residencies and will render them more desirable than any yet offered to the public. Advantageous terms will be given to the Builders in respect of the period of entry, advances of money, if required, and other points.'

Top: Blacket Place.

Above: Plaque at Sciennes Hill House where a young Walter Scott met Robert Burns in 1786.

Adam Ferguson

Born in Logierait in Perthshire, Adam Ferguson (1723–1816), a Gaelic speaker, gave up his post at the Advocates Library in 1759 to become Professor of Natural Philosophy at the University of Edinburgh, and later Professor of Pneumatics (philosophy of mind) and Moral Philosophy in 1764. In 1767 he published his famous Enlightenment text, *An Essay on Civil Society*, a work based on his observation that humans are by their very nature social beings and thus have moral belief systems that result from a social life. He resigned his Chair in 1785 to write up his lectures, published in 1792 under the title of *Principles of Moral and Political Science*. His successor in the Chair was Dugald Stewart. He died at St Andrews and is buried there in the cathedral grounds.

Blackwood's Edinburgh Magazine (1817) and David Brewster's *Edinburgh Encyclopaedia*. In 1831, he moved from Salisbury Road to 3 Ainslie Place, where he died three years later.

Many buildings pre-date the core Blacket area development, such as the front-gardened villas on **MINTO STREET** (1803–30) and the 19th-century villas (c.1817) on the north side of **MIDDLEBY STREET**. The pleasing single-storey houses with Greek Doric door pieces on the south side of Middleby Street were built in the 1820s. Miss Margaret Bancks of Middleby Street was the only female entrant in a competition run by the Royal Society of Arts in 1832 'for the best communication on a method of printing for the blind'. Miss Bancks presented 'An Alphabet and Description, with specimens of a mode of Printing for the blind' in 1832; the gold medal was eventually given to Dr Edmund Fry MD, of London.

One of the most influential mapmaking firms in the world was based at the **EDINBURGH GEOGRAPHICAL INSTITUTE**, located at 12 Duncan Street. The Bartholomew dynasty started with George, who served his apprenticeship with Daniel Lizars in Edinburgh, before setting up as a map engraver in 1826. His son, John Bartholomew Senior, was the second of six generations in the mapmaking dynasty that put Scotland and the world literally on the map. The grand portico (1815) by Thomas Hamilton was saved from Falcon Hall in Morningside at its demolition and added to the Geographical Institute building. Its grand coupled

Benjamin Bell, surgeon
As 'father of the Edinburgh Surgical School', Benjamin Bell was the most sought-after surgeon in the country, prompting his partner in practice, Andrew Wardrop, to state 'at one time nobody could die contented without having consulted Benjamin Bell'. He was a founder member of the Royal Society of Edinburgh in 1783. His *System of Surgery* (1783–88) was the first comprehensive surgical textbook in the English language and one of the most successful books published by Charles Elliot, with extensive sales in Britain, Europe and America. Bell's great-grandson, Joseph Bell, was the prototype for the fictional character of Sherlock Holmes.

columns with classical Corinthian and Tower of the Winds capitals can still be admired today.

The centrepiece of the core Blacket Estate on the east side of Minto Street was **NEWINGTON HOUSE**, Benjamin Bell's home (1805, demolished 1960s), but he had little time to enjoy it, dying there in 1806. His son, George, then commissioned James Gillespie Graham to create a plan for the estate, complete with gated entrances and porter lodges. The lodges and stone pillars (1825) at the Minto Street and Dalkeith Road ends of Blacket Avenue and Mayfield Terrace are still visible. Gillespie's plan obliged all Blacket feuars to erect houses with a minimum valuation of £600, so ensuring the exclusivity and amenity of the estate.

ARTHUR LODGE (1827–30), the most distinguished classical building in the estate, was built as Salisbury Cottage, most likely to a design by Thomas Hamilton. The house was built for Robert Mason, a builder. On his bankruptcy in 1830, the city treasurer, David Cunningham (who had employed Hamilton on the George IV Bridge and the High School projects), bought the property. Until 1841, when Major James Arthur bought and renamed the house, it was known as Salisbury Cottage. Other celebrated previous owners include the brewer Andrew Usher and explorer William Gordon Burn-Murdoch. A large globe, the South Pole uppermost on the globe, once stood in Burn-Murdoch's study in Arthur Lodge, where it was signed by eminent visitors, including polar explorers Roald Amundsen and Robert Falcon Scott.

Opposite (top): Middleby Street, south side, built c. 1827.

Opposite (bottom): Pencheck staircase in West Newington House.

Above left: The grand portico (1815) at the Edinburgh Geographical Institute, now private accommodation.

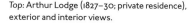

Top: Arthur Lodge (1827–30; private residence), exterior and interior views.

Above left: Benjamin Franklin, who visited Edinburgh in 1759 and 1771.

Above right: Prestonfield House, home of Sir Alexander Dick.

PRESTONFIELD HOUSE (1680s), with its twin gable-ends linked by a balcony across the entrance, was originally built for Sir James Dick, 1st Bt, Lord Provost of Edinburgh. Later Sir Alexander Dick (1703–85) physician and President of the Royal College of Physicians, hosted Allan Ramsay, David Hume, Boswell and Johnson, and Benjamin Franklin at Prestonfield. He also made many improvements to the estate and in 1774 was awarded the Gold Medal of the Royal Society of Arts for his cultivation of a strain of rhubarb for medicinal use. Benjamin Franklin sent one of his famous Franklin Stoves to Sir Alexander and another to Lord Kames. In 1816 the circular stables at Prestonfield were built by James Gillespie Graham for Sir Robert Dick.

'The loch's bearin'!' was the call to **DUDDINGSTON LOCH** for skating, and the inspiration for one of the most iconic portraits in the Scottish National Gallery, *The Reverend Robert Walker Skating on Duddingston Loch* (1795, Sir Henry Raeburn). The world's first skating club, the Edinburgh Skating Club, was formed around 1742 as a male-only elitist club, with membership by election. Later, applicants were required to skate a complete circle on each foot, then jump over first one hat, then two hats, then three hats, each on top of the other.

The loch was also used for curling and in 1825 the Duddingston Curling Club commissioned W.H. Playfair to build the unusual octagonal tower east of the loch for the storage of curling stones. The tower was known as **THOMSON'S TOWER** after local minister and landscape artist the Reverend John Thomson (1778–1840), who used its upper storey as an art studio. Thomson called the tower 'Edinburgh', so that his housekeeper could deflect unwelcome callers by stating emphatically that the minister was in 'Edinburgh'. Thomson entertained many artists and literati at his manse, including Sir Walter Scott, Francis Jeffrey, William Clerk of Eldin, David Brewster, James Hogg and Henry Cockburn. His artistic friends included Sir David Wilkie, William Bell Scott, Sir Henry Raeburn and David Scott. However his most famous guest was J.M.W. Turner, who visited the manse while working on illustrations for Scott's *Provincial Antiquities and Picturesque Scenery of Scotland*, published in ten parts between 1819 and 1826. Thomson never got a single compliment on his own work from Turner, who often chose to ignore an impressive canvas to give unstinted admiration to the frame. However, on one occasion, on leaving the manse by Duddingston Loch, he turned to Thomson and said: 'By God though, I envy you that piece of water!'

Top: Thomson's Tower, Duddingston.

Middle: Duddingston Loch in the early 19th century from Thomas Shepherd's *Modern Athens* (1829).

Below: The Earl of Moira, by John Kay.

West of Duddingston Loch is the site of the **EDINBURGH AND DALKEITH (OR 'INNOCENT') RAILWAY**, built by civil engineer and astronomer James Jardine, a close friend of Thomas Telford.

Beyond Duddingston sits one of the grandest 18th-century villas in Edinburgh, **DUDDINGSTON HOUSE**, the only classical country house in Scotland designed by Sir William Chambers (1763) and the only one to survive unaltered. It was built for James Hamilton, 8th Earl of Abercorn. He acquired the lands of Easter and Wester Duddingston in 1747 and 1767 from Andrew Fletcher, Lord Milton, and Archibald, 3rd Duke of Argyll. A later resident was the Earl of Moira who, in 1803, was appointed commander-in-chief of the army in Scotland. On 12 August

Above left: Duddingston House, Corinthian capital.

Above right: Duddingston Manse, home of the painter the Rev. John Thomson.

Right: Newhailes House, home of Sir David Dalrymple, Lord Hailes (1726–92).

Below: Lord Hailes, by John Kay

1805, after the regular militia and volunteers had fired a feu-de-joie on Portobello sands, the earl was reported to have given 'a grand entertainment' at Duddingston House.

Nearby is the great 18th-century intellectual retreat of **NEWHAILES HOUSE**, now owned by the National Trust for Scotland. The original house was built by James Smith (c.1686) and its most famous resident was Sir David Dalrymple, Lord Hailes, author of *The Annals of Scotland* (1743). The extensive library of some 7,000 volumes belonging to Lord Hailes drew praise from Samuel Johnson, who called it 'the most learned room in Europe'. David Hume once asked to borrow a copy of *The Life of Oliver Cromwell* from the library because he could not find one in the Advocates Library. Alexander Carlyle wrote of Lord Hailes after his death in 1792: 'He was well known to be of high rank in the republic of letters, and his loss will be deeply felt through many of her departments.'

Places to Visit

Many places mentioned in the text are private residences which have no, or restricted, public access. The following galleries and museums, however, are open to the public and contain much that is relevant to the history and culture of Enlightenment Edinburgh. Check websites for opening hours and special exhibitions.

_____

The Georgian House
(a restored New Town house with fine collections of furniture, paintings, silver and porcelain)

7 Charlotte Square
Edinburgh, EH2 4DR
National Trust for Scotland (NTS)

Admission charge
www.nts.org.uk

_____

Huntly House Museum
(displays of iconic objects from the city's past in a series of historic rooms)

142 Canongate
Edinburgh EH8 8DD

Free admission
www.edinburghmuseums.org.uk

Newhailes
(a grand Palladian house once owned by Sir David Dalrymple, Lord Hailes, who entertained many Enlightenment figures here)

Musselburgh, EH21 6RY
National Trust for Scotland (NTS)

Admission charge
www.nts.org.uk

_____

National Gallery of Scotland
(one of the best collections of fine art in the world)

The Mound, Edinburgh, EH2 2EL

Free admission; charge for some exhibitions
www.nationalgalleries.org

_____

National Museum of Scotland
(see especially 'Scotland Transformed' displays in the Scottish galleries)

Chambers Street
Edinburgh EH1 1JF

Free admission; charge for some exhibitions
www.nms.ac.uk

The People's Story
(explores the lives of Edinburgh's ordinary people from
the late 18th century onwards)

163 Canongate
Edinburgh EH8 8BN

Free admission
www.edinburghmuseums.org.uk

———————————

Scottish National Portrait Gallery
(come face to face with many Enlightenment characters)

1 Queen Street, Edinburgh, EH2 1JD

Free admission; charge for some exhibitions
www.nationalgalleries.org

———————————

Surgeons' Hall Museums
(noteworthy displays on 18th- and 19th-century
medicine)

Nicolson Street
Edinburgh, EH8 9DW

Admission charge
www.rcsed.ac.uk

The Writers' Museum
(a celebration of the lives of Robert Burns, Sir Walter Scott
and Robert Louis Stevenson)

Lady Stair's Close
Edinburgh EH1 2PA

Free admission
www.edinburghmuseums.org.uk

———————————

In September each year certain buildings of architectural
and cultural interest are open to the public.
See: www.doorsopendays.org.uk

Information on Edinburgh's World Heritage site is
available at: www.ewht.org.uk

Further Reading

Anderson, R.D., Lynch, M., Phillipson, N., *The University of Edinburgh: An Illustrated History, 1582–Present* (EUP, 2003)

Broadie, A., *The Scottish Enlightenment* (Birlinn Ltd, 2007)

Broadie, A., *The Cambridge Companion to the Scottish Enlightenment* (Cambridge University Press, 2003)

Brown, I.G., *David Hume: 'My Own Life'* (Royal Society of Edinburgh, 2015)

Buchan, J., *Capital of the Mind: How Edinburgh Changed the World* (Birlinn Ltd, 2003)

Buchan, J., Adam *Smith and the Pursuit of Liberty* (Profile Books, 2007)

Byrom, C., *The Edinburgh New Town Gardens: 'Blessings as well as Beauties'* (Birlinn Ltd, 2005)

Carley, M., Dalziel, R., Dargan, P. and Laird, S., *Edinburgh New Town: A Model City* (Amberley, 2015)

Cockburn, H., *Memorials of his Time*, 1856 (Kessinger Publishing, 2010)

Colvin, H.M., *A Biographical Dictionary of British Architects 1600–1840* (Yale University Press, 2008)

Cosh, M., *Edinburgh: The Golden Age* (Birlinn Ltd, 2014)

Cruft, K. and Fraser, A. (eds), *James Craig 1744–95* (Mercat Press, 1995)

Daiches, D., *Edinburgh* (Hamish Hamilton, 1978)

Daiches, D., Jones, J. and Jones, P. (eds), *A Hotbed of Genius: the Scottish Enlightenment 1730–90* (Saltire Society, 1996)

Davie, G.E., *The Scottish Enlightenment* (The Historical Association, 1981)

Devine, T.M., and J.R. Young (eds), *Eighteenth Century Scotland: New Perspectives* (Tuckwell Press, 1999)

Dingwall, H., *A Famous and Flourishing Society: The History of the Royal College of Surgeons of Edinburgh, 1505–2005* (EUP, 2005)

Edinburgh Bookshelf at *www.edinburghbookshelf.org.uk* has a searchable collection of books and pictures about the history of Edinburgh

Fraser, A.G., *The Building of Old College: Adam, Playfair and the University of Edinburgh* (EUP, 1989)

Gifford, J., McWilliam, C. and Walker, D., *Edinburgh* (Pevsner Architectural Guides: Buildings of Scotland) (Penguin Books, 1984)

Lewis, A., *The Builders of Edinburgh's New Town 1767–95* (Spire Books, 2014)

Maitland, W., *The History of Edinburgh* (Edinburgh, 1753)

McCrae, M., *Physicians and Society: A History of the Royal College of Physicians of Edinburgh* (John Donald, 2007)

McKean, C., *Edinburgh: Portrait of a City* (Century, 1991)

Milne, H.M., *Boswell's Edinburgh Journals 1767–1786* (John Donald, 2013)

Phillipson, N., *David Hume: The Philosopher as Historian* (Penguin, 2011)

Phillipson, N., *Adam Smith: An Enlightened Life* (Penguin, 2011)

Shepherd, T.H., *Modern Athens, Displayed in a series of views: or Edinburgh in the nineteenth Century* London, Jones & Co., 1831) (1st edition 1829)

Sher, R.B., *The Enlightenment and the Book* (University of Chicago, 2010)

Stevenson, R.L., *Edinburgh: Picturesque Notes* (Salamander Press, 1983)

Whyte, Iain, *Scotland and the Abolition of Black Slavery 1756–1838* (EUP, 2006)

Youngson, A.J., *The Making of Classical Edinburgh* (EUP, 1966)

Index